ISRAELI STORIES

*a selection of
the best contemporary
Hebrew writing*

edited by JOEL BLOCKER
introduction by ROBERT ALTER

SCHOCKEN BOOKS · NEW YORK

ACKNOWLEDGMENTS

For permission to include several stories in this collection acknowledgment is due: *Partisan Review* for "The Sermon"; *Israel Argosy,* The Jewish Agency, Jerusalem, for "Tehilah" and "The Name"; and Karni Publishers Ltd., Tel Aviv, for "A Roll of Canvas." I am grateful to Mrs. Sylvia Landress and the staff of the Zionist Library and Archives, The Jewish Agency, New York, for their generous assistance. To S. Y. Agnon, Meir Mindlin, Moshe Kohn, and Yehuda Amihai, my heartfelt thanks for their encouragement and inspiration. I wish to record here, too, my debt to Shmuel and Rina Barcay, without whom this book would not have been possible.   –J. B.

Library of Congress Catalog Card Number 61-14918
ISBN 0-8052-0108-4

Manufactured in the United States of America
BVG 01

Preface

Israel today is a land overflowing with writers and readers. But modern Hebrew literature goes back barely more than two hundred years, and much of the early work was either nonfiction or so didactic that it was actually fiction only in form. Serious Hebrew writing about life in Palestine-Israel has existed, of course, only as long as there has been a significant Jewish community there, no more than sixty years. Until the last decade, its potential audience was never larger than five-hundred-thousand, its actual readership much less.

The establishment and rapid growth of the State radically altered the status of Hebrew literature in two major respects: First, by providing an official stamp the State in effect transformed Hebrew writing, ready or not, into a national literature. Second, and more important, the State's remarkable ability to assimilate large numbers of immigrants into a Hebrew-speaking culture within a short period has given its writers a real audience for the first time. Many Israeli authors have only recently experienced the pleasure of *not* knowing their readers personally.

Through most of its history, however, modern Hebrew literature was sustained by a relatively small group. In comparison with nineteenth- and twentieth-century Yiddish fiction, which always had a large following among the Jewish masses in Eastern Europe, Hebrew writing was a coterie literature. Quantitatively, it managed to produce an impressive body of work, which is a tribute to the fecundity and tenaciousness of its devotees. Yet qualitatively Hebrew literature long suffered from its initial failure to establish a mass base, and the effects of this continue to be felt today.

The *Haskalah* (Enlightenment) writers who inaugurated the modern Hebrew renaissance in the nineteenth century were predominantly social-minded. They sought the emancipation of East European Jews through communal and religious reform and, especially, through education. Their characteristic literary tone was pedagogic and hortatory. For many Israeli writers, literature is still primarily educational and inspirational; esthetic and moral considerations have remained secondary.

Zionism, which replaced the *Haskalah* around the turn of the century as the dominant force in Hebrew culture, had a similar, though even more pronounced, effect on Hebrew literature. For the Hebrew writers of the period Zionism was not merely a political credo calling for a return to the Jewish homeland. It was a revolutionary ideology, embracing all areas of life, which preached total emancipation from ultimate communal extinction in exile. From 1910 to 1948 Hebrew prose strove faithfully to record the struggle of the burgeoning Jewish community in Palestine. Its aims were identical with those of the people whose progress it was attempting to document. The writer surrendered to history; his critical function was largely abandoned. Inevitably, too, literature was politicized. And since most writers, like most of their countrymen, chose to identify themselves with one particular coloration in the multi-hued political spectrum that existed in Palestine (and still exists in Israel), their work was not only broadly ideological but often narrowly partisan. The difference between the mightiness of history and the pettiness of party propaganda proved in many cases to be very small.

Fortunately, this is not the whole of the matter. As the nine stories that follow indicate, and as Robert Alter's appreciation makes clear, there is a good deal more to contemporary Israeli writing than mere ideological posturing. True, none of the writers included is untouched by ideology; each in his own way is committed to basic Zionist beliefs. Yet all reflect in their work not a simple mirroring but an ordered criticism of the life around them. "This is a Jewish trait too," says a character in one of the stories, ". . . to believe with perfect faith, with the mad and burning faith of all the heart and all the soul, and yet somehow *not* to believe, the least little bit—and to let this tiny bit be decisive. . . ."

In keeping with Israel's diverse literature, no single image of the country is projected here. Nor, in fact, were the stories even chosen for their "representative" qualities. They represent nothing more than what the editor considers a fair sampling of the best contemporary Israeli writing, and were selected simply on the basis of literary merit. In contrast to some recent popular fiction, of both American and Israeli origin, they do not

7

attempt to explain what life is like on a kibbutz, how it feels to be an attractive young woman drafted into an army of Middle Eastern he-men, or, least of all, why six-hundred-thousand Jews were able to defeat forty million Arabs and establish a viable modern state. A tough-minded ideology can too easily be distorted into popular myth and fantasy. Hopefully, above and beyond their primary literary intentions, these stories will serve to correct some current misconceptions and debased notions about Zionism and the State.

A final word about the translations: Special care has been taken to avoid the archaisms and crudities of language which in the past have often vitiated Hebrew literature in English. Five of the translations were specifically commissioned for this volume; of the remaining four, three have never appeared in book form before. Except for a few distinctly Jewish words or phrases and an occasional expression in Arabic, an English equivalent has in every case been found. Freed of its artificial quaintness, I believe, Hebrew prose can be enjoyed and evaluated like any other modern literature.

JOEL BLOCKER

New York, August 1962

CONTENTS

Introduction

The present volume of Israeli stories reassuringly illustrates the other half of a frequently asserted half-truth. Modern Hebrew literature, it is claimed, like Yiddish literature, does not really share the large concerns of serious literary activity in the West. The Hebrew writer ordinarily does not address himself to the human situation with all its far-reaching possibilities of tragedy or comedy, but to the Jewish situation, which is quite another thing. Consequently, Hebrew and Yiddish writers—so goes the claim—develop a system of typology rather than methods of characterization, for they are most essentially interested in the Jewish people, its particular qualities and its present fate or ultimate destiny, while the individual, who is central in other modern literatures, stands at the periphery of their vision.

And it is true that when one looks back over the last

century of Hebrew letters, the looming question posed by the stories and novels and poems is often "What does it mean to be a Jew?" rather than "What does it mean to be a man?" This narrowing of focus is quite understandable. During the nineteenth and early twentieth centuries in central and eastern Europe, creating a secular literature in Hebrew was itself a defiant act of cultural rebellion or even nationalist self-assertion. From the time of the Enlightenment, literary activity in Hebrew was the major expression of a secularist cultural renaissance among Jews; by late nineteenth century, it was also intimately linked with—or perhaps had even led to—Zionist nationalism. It is hardly surprising, then, that so many of the European-born Hebrew writers should be absorbed in pondering the state of the Jewish people and the future of Jewish culture, sometimes to the exclusion of other subject matter and often to the detriment of their literary art.

This cultural self-consciousness of modern Hebrew literature is a matter of history. On the other hand, the collection of stories offered here is largely a matter of current events—all the stories are the fruit of the last few years—and a significant change has taken place. The older literary generation is represented by its two most prominent members, S. Y. Agnon and Haim Hazaz; each, in a very different way, marks the end of the European-nurtured tradition of Hebrew literature. The six younger contributors to the volume, all either Israeli-born or childhood immigrants to the new land, have other concerns, though one of them devotes a story to the pain of separation from the Diaspora's long continuity of Jewish life.

In a sense, the two pieces by S. Y. Agnon included in this collection epitomize the transition from the old Hebrew fiction to the new: they show a Janus-faced

Agnon looking back wistfully at a luminous Jewish past and looking out unflinchingly on a twentieth-century reality in which attitudes toward all traditional values tend to be ambivalent. On the surface, Agnon's "Tehilah" would seem to belong to that gallery of quaint and loving portraits of quaint and loveable types which one naturally associates with Hebrew and, more particularly, with Yiddish literature. But Tehilah is clearly much more to the narrator than a charming and curious folk type. She is the last representative of a world which has passed; she exemplifies what is for Agnon the unique greatness of that departed world—its ability to transform everyday existence into a sustained regimen of sanctity. It is characteristic of Agnon's sense of past and present that Tehilah has uncannily over-stayed her time in the world, for only in someone born "four or five generations ago" could Agnon envisage such saintliness. The story, therefore, is both a portrait of a saintly woman and an elegy over a vanished way of life. There are frequent allusions in the story to the wholeness of the past and the incompleteness of the present. The invalid widow complains about the "bits of stoves" people use nowadays. Tehilah mistrusts the narrator's newfangled fountain pen, and asks him to write with a quill upon old crown-paper made "when they knew how good paper was made." Tehilah's death at the end of the story is more than the obvious con-clusion of a fictional biographic sketch. Agnon, who writes always with painstaking care and meticulous control of tone and detail, ends his story with a sig-nificantly weighted image of death and abandonment. "Tehilah has left us," the narrator thinks again and again; and we infer: Tehilah, and Tehilah's world as well.

On the other hand, the world of Adiel Amzeh, in

"Forevermore," Agnon's second story, has been stripped of all the certainties, all the uncomplicated feeling for the loveliness of sanctity, that characterized the older world of Tehilah. If there is anything in this story which corresponds to the traditional sphere of holiness, it is, paradoxically, the leper colony. The equivalent to a sacred Torah-scroll in Adiel Amzeh's Jerusalem is the enigmatic book of ancient Gumlidata, covered with the suppurations of its living-dead guardians, generations of lepers, yet somehow the most precious thing in life for the protagonist. A number of details in the involved symbolic structure of the story suggest that Agnon has in mind a specifically Jewish set of referents. (To cite one key example, the hero's name means "God's-Ornament This-People.") But this "Jewish" story is also a universal one. Its concerns are not in any real sense national; for peoplehood—if the Jewish people is in fact symbolized by the lepers—has become here a metaphysical concept. Adiel Amzeh's discovery of what it means to be a Jew is, at least by implication, a discovery of what it means to be a man. The reader does not have to unlock all the mysteries of the story's symbolism in order to feel in Adiel Amzeh a credible individual who has come to a crucial new awareness about the paradoxical nature of commitment, of sacrifice, of truth itself.

By contrast, Haim Hazaz's story, "The Sermon," is very much in the tradition of Hebrew fiction dedicated to the exploration of national issues; or perhaps, it could be a final gesture of that tradition—for the clear implication of the protagonist's position is that henceforth there will be no grounds or need for Jewish self-questioning. We should be quick, however, to remind ourselves that the angry Yudka's wholesale rejection of Jewish history is the argument of a character in a story, not of an essay by Hazaz. Yudka—the name suggests "little Jew"—represents one pole of a dialectic Hazaz has been carrying on within himself about the Zionist state and its real or imagined continuity with Jewish history. While Yudka's creator has endowed him with a great deal of keen insight and a strong distaste for self-delusion, he is also a character whose passionate nature and limitations of knowledge lead him to sweeping over-statements. Hazaz has shown himself in his recent novels to be a thorough-going secular Zionist and an uncompromising opponent of the transcendental emphases in Jewish experience, but he also holds the standard Zionist position that Israel should mean a normalization of Jewish life, not a clean break with it; so it would seem that Yudka is more a devil's advocate for Hazaz than his spokesman.

In any case, the question of what or how a Jew should be is still central in Hazaz's work, while it does not occupy the younger writers in the same way. They are —like so many Jews in other parts of the world— troubled about their Jewishness, but the dilemma of Jewish existence is not often the main focus of their writing. In this collection, it is the theme of only one story by a younger writer—Aharon Megged's "The Name." And the episode Megged relates is in the nature of a final, sad pronouncement on the subject— it hardly leads to further considerations. The young Israeli couple in the story are forced to realize the unbridgeable chasm that separates them from their grandfather and his world: the story ends, like "Tehilah," on a note of abandonment and orphanhood.

This theme of cultural disinheritance does recur among the writings of the native Israelis. It is in fact a major point of discussion in S. Yizhar's long novel, *The Days of Ziklag,* the book which many of Israel's younger intellectuals regard as the most embracing spiritual inventory yet taken of their generation. It should also be clear, however, that the lament over being severed from the past has its limitations as a subject for fiction, and an exclusive concentration on it would reflect little more than surrender to self-pity. Fortunately, it is by no means the chief subject of the younger Hebrew writers. The fulfillment of the Zionist ideal of a "normalized" Jewish life seems to be bringing about a healthy kind of normalization of Hebrew literature as well. The young Israeli setting out to write fiction does not usually begin by mulling over the fate of his people or its future. Quite like any young American or French or British writer, he finds himself a distinct individual troubled with problems or moved by beauty or excited by the newness of experience, and he attempts to transcribe this individual vision of reality into fiction. The fact that he speaks Hebrew and lives in the land where the Bible was created has no particular hold on his imagination because he has always spoken Hebrew and he has always lived in this country. The feeling is concretely expressed by Yosef Gretz, the hero of Yoram Kaniuk's poignant account of Tel Aviv boyhood: "Now the city races after us, the wasteland retreats and I shout 'Ayyy,' because I was born here. If I had been born in Germany, I would say 'aow,' in America, 'ouch.' Here dreams are buried. . . ." And it is the business of the writer, who takes his national identity for granted, not to worry over the cultural significance of the "Ayyy" he naturally shouts, but to unearth the buried dreams —something which Kaniuk does with considerable effectiveness.

To an American reader, it may not seem particularly noteworthy that Israeli writers are now doing what serious writers all over the world generally do. But if one considers the circumstances in which a young Israeli writes, one must admire his integrity and his firmness of resolution. In a new state surrounded by enemies, compelled to keep up a large military establishment, one might expect the literary output to be marred by frequent displays of well-meaning patriotism or misguided chauvinism. For while the young Hebrew writer may be doing his best simply to probe with honesty and intelligence the reality in which he is immersed, something more is often expected from him—by many critics, by some older writers, by the press, by his party, by government figures. In the spring of 1962, for example, at the festive twentieth convention of the Hebrew Writers' Association, the young novelists and poets were assaulted from two sides. The convention began with a message from the prime minister sharply criticizing Hebrew writers for their lack of social responsibility, for their failure to further through their work the great national effort of the Ingathering of Exiles. Then Hazaz, who as the creator of the iconoclast Yudka should have known better, delivered an opening address in which he attacked with equal vehemence the young writers for turning their backs on the riches of Jewish tradition, and the Israeli public for its indifference to Hebrew books.

It is true, of course, that Hebrew literature must struggle to keep its own footing in the tide of translated culture that floods its relatively tiny reading audience. But in point of fact, the indigenous literature of Israel has often seemed pale and uninteresting not because its writers failed to be authentically Jewish, as Hazaz suggests, but because they had not yet found adequate ways to be themselves in literature. The stories in this volume offer two encouraging indications: first, that the younger Hebrew writers are trying to find out what they can or should expect of themselves instead of attempting to produce what others may expect of them; second, that the younger writers are beginning to discover distinctive voices for their personal needs of expression.

War, or a political situation tantamount to war, is the background for four of the six stories by younger writers in this collection. It is significant that in every case war is merely a background, while what the writer is really concerned with is human beings and their moral problems or inner life. In Moshe Shamir's "The Next of Kin," the deadly tension between Arab and Jew is purely tangential to the main concern of the story. Shamir is interested in exploring a very different kind of tension—that generated among people by a conflict of love. A fatal border incident allows Shamir to set up the situation he wants, but almost any other form of sudden death would have done as well.

Benjamin Tammuz's "A Roll of Canvas," set against the antagonisms that marked the last years of the Mandate in Palestine, is a study in divided allegiances and moral growth. The story really has two centers of interest: Pesach Katz, the brave and pitiful little man with a sensitive conscience, and the young narrator through whose eyes we see Katz. Pesach Katz's quixotic efforts to express his convictions in action attract our sympathy because they suggest the plight of so many people in our world struggling to remain independent moral entities while spun about in a swirl of forces beyond their control. And the partisan Israeli youngster who tells us about Katz learns something from him, too. Although he is ostensibly scornful of the naive little fellow who writes poetry and abhors violence, he is obviously fascinated by him as well. Pesach Katz represents another order of moral awareness, and the narrator who wonderingly observes the older man is forced to realize the bias and limitation of his own sense of life.

The problem suggested by Tammuz's story, the assertion of individual conscience in the face of a historical situation which threatens to extinguish it, has become an important theme of Israeli fiction in recent years. The War of Independence and the later Sinai Campaign, far from being objects of glorification for the serious Hebrew writers, often appear in their work as oppressive memories: many of the stories and novels are haunted by the terror of a situation in which the individual is called on to murder in the name of the state. The recollection of this traumatic experience stalks after the hero of Kaniuk's novel, *The Acrophile*. The same trauma in Megged's *As It Happeneth to the Fool* sets off the major moral crisis in the protagonist. And this danger of the obliteration of conscience by war is a central theme in Yizhar's *The Days of Ziklag* as it is in his story, "The Prisoner," included in this volume. In both the novel and the story, the impact on Yizhar of the Sartre school of existentialism is clearly detectable. In a meaningless world wholly indifferent to human enterprise, the individual must be courageous enough to assume complete responsibility for his own moral decisions, as if—in Sartre's terms—he were deciding each time for all mankind. "It's a big day," whispers a voice within the protagonist of "The Prisoner." "It's a day of rebellion. It's the day when, at last, you have the choice in your hands. And you hold the power to decide."

The most original protest against the demoralizing effect of war in this group of stories, at least from a technical point of view, is Yehuda Amihai's "The Battle for the Hill." The dreamlike progress of the narrative, its willful employment of absurd detail, effectively suggests the way war radically disrupts normal life and destroys order and meaning. Amihai's soldiers scurry back and forth, swept up in the vortex of activity for its own sake which seems to be an inevitable part of military operations, changing "short pants for long, and long for short," making frantic and useless preparations for a battle that never takes place. Telling use is made of surrealistic images to convey war's sudden and total expropriation of civilian existence. A well-pressed handkerchief turns into a military map. Death notices are mobilization calls in disguise. Lovers are sent to the border to make love before the enemy "for the sake of camouflage." Amihai's acrid satire, however personal in style, reflects the general embitterment of his literary contemporaries toward an armed existence to which they have been wedded by necessity.

The younger Hebrew writers clearly have attempted to confront the world in their work as individuals, not merely as members of a people. But the stories in this collection suggest the beginning of a further development in Hebrew fiction—a growing interest in exploring the possibilities of form. Israel's native writers, with all their moral integrity, have at times appeared to be bent on the pursuit of their own existential problems to the manifest neglect of the artistic shaping of their work. A decade ago, one could object with considerable justification that none of the younger novelists, except for Yizhar, had developed anything like an original style. It is significant, then, that three of the six stories by the younger generation presented here experiment with narrative technique. The experimenting has not been undertaken in the doctrinaire spirit of a self-conscious avant-garde. The stories rather indicate that their authors are seeking to manipulate the narrative medium in order to achieve as faithful a reproduction as possible of their own vision of life. These venturesome younger writers understandably are not always uniformly successful. Yizhar's interior monologue has its flats as well as its flashes of insight and its lyrical heights. Amihai's fragmentation of narrative unity, for all its striking moments, is not without some *longeurs*. By contrast, Kaniuk seems able to sustain more consistently the lyric freshness of his wide-eyed child narrator in "The Parched Earth." But all three writers, in whatever varying ways, have learned how to convey a livelier, more particular and immediate sense of their world than earlier Israeli fiction was able to achieve. Yizhar gives his story a convincing local habitation because he can use poetic language to evoke the distinctive Mediterranean setting of his native land.

> Everything hummed of summer, like a golden beehive. A whirlpool of gleaming mountain-fields, olive hills, and a sky ablaze with an intense silence blinded us for moments and so beguiled our hearts that one longed for a word of redeeming joy.

And Kaniuk succeeds in making words transmit his own sensitive response to Tel Aviv's transition from haunting desertland to the prosaic reality of a modern city.

> My marvelous city, my wonderful city, my city of empty lots. They are filling your emptiness. . . . One house, then another. They bring death to the lots. The wild visions of pioneers roasting potatoes in the wilderness, and a people becoming its own Messiah, turn into a reality of balconies. Old Rabinowitz, along with young Rabinowitz, paints his balcony the color of the murder of the beautiful wastelands. The wasteland cries. How sad the cry of the wasteland in the mouths of jackals at night: yuhuuuuuuu.

This determination of the younger Israeli writers to remain as faithful as possible in their work to the immediacy of personal experience has one noteworthy concomitant: in the fiction they are producing one can also find a greater degree of fidelity to the common cultural experience of life in the State of Israel. For literary style is more than the expression of the writer's personality; it is the expression of a personality embedded in a specific cultural milieu. As writers like Yizhar, Kaniuk, Amihai, and (in his most recent work) Megged discover the artistic means to speak for themselves, they are also speaking more effectively for their culture. At their best—as the two passages cited above may suggest—these younger Hebrew writers are able to capture in their fiction the new rhythms and resonances, the nuances of thought and feeling, that make life in Israel distinctively Israeli.

Cambridge, Mass.   ROBERT ALTER
June, 1962

Tehilah

Shmuel Yosef Agnon was born in 1888 in Galicia, the southernmost district of Poland, then part of the Austro-Hungarian empire. He received a traditional religious education and, at the age of twenty, left home for Palestine. In 1912 Agnon was back in Europe; the rootless, restless years that followed, spent mostly in Germany, saw him living in Berlin, Munich, Leipzig, Wiesbaden and Homburg. With his return to Palestine in 1925 his period of mature creativity began. Now in his seventies, he continues to live and write in Jerusalem, a city whose religious and mystical associations provide endless grist for his imagination.

Agnon's novels, stories and novellas, which have appeared so far in eleven volumes, have become classics of Hebrew literature in his lifetime. Three of his books have been translated into English: the novel The Bridal Canopy (1935); the novella In the Heart of the Seas (1948); and Days of Awe, a collection of oral and written legends pertaining to the Jewish High Holy Days. "Tehilah," which in addition to being a proper name is the Hebrew word meaning "praise" or "psalm," is one of Agnon's Jerusalem tales. The poverty-stricken Jewish community of the old walled city, with its remote otherworldliness, is no longer in existence; it was destroyed in the Arab-Israeli war of 1948.

Now there used to be in Jerusalem a certain old woman, as comely an old woman as you have seen in your days. Righteous she was, and wise she was, and gracious and humble: for kindness and pity were the light of her eyes, and every wrinkle in her face told of blessing and peace. I know that women should not be likened to angels: yet her would I liken to an angel of God. She had in her, besides, the vigor of youth; so that she wore old age like a mantle, while in herself there was seen no trace of her years.

Until I had left Jerusalem she was quite unknown to me; only upon my return did I come to know her. If you ask why I never heard of her before, I shall answer: Why have you not heard of her until now? It is appointed for every man to meet whom he shall meet, and the time for this, and the fitting occasion. It happened that I had gone to visit one of Jerusalem's noted men of learning, who lived near the Wailing Wall. Having failed to find his house, I came upon a woman who was going by with a pail of water, and I asked her the way.

She said, "Come with me, I will show you."

I replied, "Do not trouble yourself. Tell me the way, and I shall go on alone."

She answered, smiling, "What is it to you if an old woman should earn herself a *mitzvah?**"

"If it be a *mitzvah,*" said I, "then do so; but give me this pail that you carry."

She smiled again and said, "If I do as you ask, it will make the *mitzvah* but a small one."

"It is only the trouble I wish to be small, and not the merit of your deed," I said.

She answered, "This is no trouble at all, but a privi-

---

* *Mitzvah:* Literally, a commandment; a moral duty that confers spiritual reward.

lege; since the Holy One has furnished his creatures with hands that they may supply all their needs."

We made our way amongst the stones and through the alleys, avoiding the camels and the asses, the drawers of water and the idlers and the gossip-mongers, until she halted and said, "Here is the house of him you seek."

I found the man of learning at home at his desk. Whether he recognized me at all is doubtful; for he had just made an important discovery, which he at once began to relate. As I took my leave I thought to ask him who that woman might be, whose face shone with such peace and whose voice was so gentle and calm. But there is no interrupting a scholar when he speaks of his latest discovery.

Some days later I went again to the Old City, this time to visit the aged widow of a rabbi; for I had promised her grandson before my return that I would attend to her welfare.

That day marked the beginning of the rainy season. Already the rain was falling, and the sun was obscured by clouds. In other lands this would have seemed like a normal day of spring; but here in Jerusalem, which is pampered with constant sunshine through seven or eight months of the year, we think it is winter should the sun once fail to shine with all its strength, and we hide ourselves in houses and courtyards, or in any place that affords a sheltering roof.

I walked alone and free, smelling the good smell of the rain as it fell exultantly, wrapping itself in mist, and heightening the tints of the stones, and beating at the walls of houses, and dancing on roofs, and making great pools beneath that were sometimes turbid and sometimes gleamed in the sunbeams that intermittently broke through the clouds to view the work of the waters—

for in Jerusalem even on a rainy day the sun yet seeks to perform its task.

Turning in between the shops with their arched doorways at the street of the smiths, I went on past the shoemakers, and the blanket-weavers, and the little stalls that sell hot broths, till I came to the Street of the Jews. Huddled in their tattered rags sat the beggars, not caring even to reach a hand from their cloaks, and glowering sullenly at each man who passed without giving them money. I had with me a purse of small coins, and went from beggar to beggar distributing them. Finally I asked for the house of the *rabbanit,** and they told me the way.

I entered a courtyard, one of those which to a casual passer-by seems entirely deserted, and after mounting six or seven broken flights of stairs, came to a warped door. Outside I stumbled against a cat, and within a heap of rubbish stood in my way. Because of the mist I could not see anyone, but I heard a faint, apprehensive voice calling, "Who is there?" Looking up, I now made out a kind of iron bed submerged in a wave of pillows and bolsters, and in the depths of the wave an alarmed and agitated old woman.

I introduced myself, saying that I was recently come from abroad with greetings from her grandson. She put out a hand from under the bedding to draw the coverlet up to her chin, saying, "Tell me now, does he own many houses, and does he keep a maidservant, and has he fine carpets in every room?" Then she sighed, "This cold will be the death of me."

Seeing that she was so irked with the cold, it occurred to me that a kerosene stove might give her some ease: so I thought of a little stratagem.

"Your grandson," I said, "has entrusted me with a

---

* *Rabbanit:* A form of address meaning "rabbi's wife."

small sum of money to buy you a stove: a portable stove that one fills with kerosene, with a wick that burns and gives off much heat." I took out my wallet and said, "See, here is the money."

In a vexed tone she answered, "And shall I go now to buy a stove, with these feet that are on me? Feet did I say? Blocks of ice I mean. This cold will drive me out of my wits if it won't drive me first to my grave, to the Mount of Olives.* And look you, abroad they say that the Land of Israel is a hot land. Hot it is, yes, for the souls in Gehenna."

"Tomorrow," I said, "the sun will shine out and make the cold pass away."

" 'Ere comfort comes, the soul succumbs.' "

"In an hour or two," I said, "I shall have sent you the stove."

She crouched down among her coverlets and bolsters, as if to show that she did not trust me as her benefactor.

I left her and walked out to the Jaffa Road. There I went to a shop that sold household goods, bought a portable stove of the best make in stock, and sent it on to the old *rabbanit*. An hour later I returned to her, thinking that, if she was unfamiliar with stoves of this kind, it would be as well to show her the method of lighting it. On the way, I said to myself: Not a word of thanks, to be sure, will I get for my pains. How different is one old woman from another! For she who showed me the way to the scholar's house is evidently kind to all comers; and this other woman will not even show kindness to those who are prompt to seek her comfort.

But here I must insert a brief apology. My aim is

---

* Before 1948, the Mount of Olives was the traditional burying ground for Jerusalem's Jews.

not to praise one woman to the detriment of others; nor, indeed, do I aspire to tell the story of Jerusalem and all its inhabitants. The range of man's vision is narrow: shall it comprehend the City of the Holy One, blessed be He? If I speak of the *rabbanit,* it is for this reason only, that at the entrance to her house it was again appointed for me to encounter the other old woman.

I bowed and made way for her; but she stood still and greeted me as warmly as one might greet one's nearest kinsman. Momentarily I was puzzled as to who she might be. Could this be one of the old women I had known in Jerusalem before leaving the country? Yet most of these, if not all, had perished of hunger in the time of the war. Even if one or two survived, I myself was much changed; for I was only a lad when I left Jerusalem, and the years spent abroad had left their mark.

She saw that I was surprised, and smiled, saying, "It seems you do not recognize me. Are you not the man who wished to carry my pail on the way to your friend's house?"

"And you are the woman," said I, "who showed me the way. Yet now I stand here bewildered, and seem not to know you."

Again she smiled. "Are you obliged, then, to remember every old woman who lives in the Old City?"

"Yet," I said, "you recognized me."

She answered, "Because the eyes of Jerusalem look out upon all Israel, each man who comes to us is engraved on our heart; thus we never forget him."

"It is a cold day," I said, "a day of wind and rain, and here I stand, keeping you out of doors."

She answered, with love in her voice, "I have seen worse cold than any we have in Jerusalem. As for wind and rain, are we not thankful? For daily we bless God, saying, 'Who causes the wind to blow and the rain to fall.' You have done a great *mitzvah:* you have put new life into old bones. The stove which you sent to the *rabbanit* is warming her, body and soul."

I hung my head, as a man does who is abashed at hearing his own praise. Perceiving this, she said:

"The doing of a *mitzvah* need not make a man bashful. Our fathers, it is true, performed so many that it was needless to publish their deeds. But we, who do less, perform a *mitzvah* even by letting the *mitzvah* be known: then others will hear, and learn from our deeds what they too must do. Now, my son, go to the *rabbanit,* and see how much warmth your *mitzvah* has brought."

I went inside and found the stove lit, and the *rabbanit* seated beside it. Light flickered from the perforated holes, and the room was full of warmth. A lean cat lay in her lap, and she was gazing at the stove and talking to the cat, saying to it, "It seems that you like this heat more than I do."

I said, "I see that the stove burns well and gives off a fine heat. Are you satisfied?"

"And if I am satisfied," said the *rabbanit,* "will that make it smell the less or warm me the more? A stove there was in my old home, that would burn from the last day of the Feast of Tabernacles to the first night of the Passover, and give off heat like the sun in the dog-days of the month of Tammuz; a lasting joy it was, not like these bits of stove which burn for a short while. But nowadays one cannot expect good workmanship. Enough it is if folk make a show of working. Yes, that is what I said to the people of our town when my dear husband, the Rabbi, passed away: may he speak for me in the world to come! When they got themselves a new rabbi, I said to them, What can you expect? Do you expect that he will be like your old rabbi? Enough it is if he starts no troubles. And so I said to the neighbors just now, when they came to see the stove that my grandson sent me through you. I said to them, 'This stove is like the times, and these times are like the stove.' What did he write to you, this grandson? Didn't write at all? Nor does he write to me. No doubt he thinks that by sending me this bit of a stove he has done his duty."

After leaving the *rabbanit,* I said to myself: I too think that by sending her this bit of a stove I have done my duty: surely there is no need to go again. Yet in the end I returned, and all because of that same gracious old woman; for this was not the last occasion that was appointed for me to see her.

Again I must say that I have no intention of recounting all that happened to me in those days. A man does many things, and if he were to describe them all he would never make an end to his story. Yet all that relates to that old woman deserves to be told.

On the eve of new moon I walked to the Wailing Wall, as we in Jerusalem are accustomed to do, to pray at the Wailing Wall at the rising of each moon.

Already most of the winter had passed, and spring blossoms had begun to appear. Up above, the heavens were pure, and the earth had put off her grief. The sun smiled in the sky; the Old City shone in its light. And we too rejoiced, despite the troubles that beset us; for these troubles were many and evil, and before we had reckoned with one, yet another came in its wake.

From Jaffa Gate as far as the Wailing Wall, men and women from all the communities of Jerusalem moved in a steady stream, together with those newcomers whom the Place* had restored to their space, albeit their space had not yet been found. But in the open space before

* The Place: the Cabalistic name for God.

the Wall, at the booth of the Mandatory Police, sat the police of the Mandate, whose function it was to see that none guarded the worshippers save only they. Our adversaries, wishing to provoke us, perceived this and set about their provocations. Those who had come to pray were herded together and driven to seek shelter close up against the stones of the Wall, some weeping and some as if dazed. And still we say, How long, O Lord? How long? For we have trodden the lowest stair of degradation, yet You tarry to redeem us.

I found a place for myself at the Wall, standing at times amongst the worshippers, at times amongst the bewildered bystanders. I was amazed at the peoples of the world: as if it were not enough that they oppressed us in all lands, yet they must also oppress us in our home.

As I stood there I was driven from my place by one of the police who carried a baton. This man was in a great rage, on account of some ailing old woman who had brought a stool with her to the Wall. The policeman sprang forward and kicked the stool, throwing the woman to the ground and confiscating the stool: for she had infringed the law enacted by the legislators of the Mandate, which forbade worshippers to bring seats to the Wall. And those who had come to pray saw this, yet held their peace: for how can right dispute against might? Then came forward the same old woman whom I knew, and looked the policeman straight in the eyes. And the policeman averted his gaze, and returned the stool to its owner.

I went up to her and said, "Your eyes have more effect than all the pledges of England. For England, which gave us the Balfour Declaration, sends her officers to annul it; while you only looked upon that wicked one, and frustrated his evil intent."

She replied, "Do not speak of him so, for he is a good gentile, who saw that I was grieved and gave back her stool to that poor woman. . . . But have you said your afternoon prayer? I ask because, if you are free, I can put in your way the *mitzvah* of visiting the sick. The *rabbanit* is now really and truly ill. If you wish, come with me and I shall take you by a short route." I joined her and we went together.

From alley to alley, from courtyard to courtyard, we made our way down, and at each step she took she would pause to give a piece of candy to a child, or a coin to a beggar, or to ask the health of a man's wife or, if it were a woman, the health of her husband. I said, "Since you are concerned with everyone's welfare, let me ask after yours."

She answered, "Blessed be the Name, for I lack nothing at his hand. The Holy One has given to each of his creatures according to its need; and I too am one of these. But today I have special cause for thanking him, for he has doubled my portion."

"How is this?" I asked.

She replied, "Each day I read the psalms appointed for the day, but today I read the psalms for two days together." Even as she spoke, her face clouded over with grief.

"Your joy has passed away," I said.

She was silent for a moment. Then she said, "Yes, my son, I was joyful, and now it is not so." Yet even as she spoke, the light shone out again from her face. She raised her eyes and said, "Blessed be He, who has turned away my sorrow."

"Why," I asked, "were you joyful, yet afterwards sad, and now, joyful again?"

She said, very gently, "Since your words are not chosen with care, I must tell you, this was not the way to ask. Rather should you have said, 'How have you deserved it, that God should turn away your sorrow?' For in his blessed eyes, all is one, whether sorrow or joy."

"Perhaps in future," said I, "my words will be chosen with care, since you teach me how one must speak. 'Happy is the man who does not forget Thee.' It is a text of much meaning."

She said, "You are a good man, and it is a good text you have told me; so I too shall not withhold good words. You asked why I was joyful, and why I was sad, and why I now rejoice. Assuredly you know as I do, that all a man's deeds are appointed, from the hour of his birth to the hour of his death; and accordingly, the number of times he shall say his psalms. But the choice is free how many psalms he will say on any one day. This man may complete the whole book in a day, and that man may say one section a day, or the psalms for each day according to the day. I have made it my custom to say each day the psalms for that day; but this morning I went on and said the psalms for two days together. When I became aware of this I was sad, lest it meant that there were no more need for me in the world, and that I was disposed of and made to finish my portion in haste. For 'it is a good thing to give thanks to the Lord'; and when I am dead I shall not be able to say one psalm, or even one word. Then the Holy One saw my grief, and showed his marvellous kindness by allowing me to know that such is his own very will. If it pleases the Name to take my life, who am I that I should grieve? Thus He at once turned away my sorrow. Blessed be He and blessed be his name."

I glanced at her, wondering to myself by what path one might come to a like submission. I thought of the men of ancient times, and their virtuous ways; I spoke to her of past generations. Then I said, "You have seen with your own eyes more than I can describe in words."

She answered, "When a person's life is prolonged for many days and years, it is granted him to see many things; good things, and yet better things."

"Tell me," I said to her, "of these same good things."

She was silent for a while; then she said, "How shall I begin? Let me start with my childhood. When I was a little girl, I was a great chatterbox. Really, from the time I stood up in the morning till the time I lay down at night, words never ceased pouring from my lips. There was an old man in our neighborhood, who said to those delighting in my chatter: 'A pity it is for this little girl; if she wastes all her words in childhood, what will be left for her old age?' I became terribly frightened, thinking this meant that I might die the very next day. But in time I came to fathom the old man's meaning, which was that a person must not use up in a short while what is allotted him for a whole lifetime. I made a habit of testing each word to see if there was real need for it to be said, and practiced a strict economy of speech. Through this economy, I saved up a great store of words, and my life has been prolonged until they are all used up. Now that only a few words remain, you ask me to speak them. If I do so it will hasten my end."

"Upon such terms," said I, "I would certainly not ask you to speak. But how is it that we keep walking and walking, yet we have still not come to the house of the *rabbanit?*"

She said, "You still have in mind those courtyards we used to take for a short cut. But now that most of the Old City has been settled by the Arabs, we must go by a roundabout way."

We approached one of these courtyards. She said, "Do you see this courtyard? Forty families of Israel once lived here, and here were two synagogues, and here in the daytime and nighttime there were study and prayer. But they left this place, and Arabs came and occupied it."

We approached a tumble-down house. She said, "Do you see this house? Here was a great academy where the scholars of the Torah lived and studied. But they left this house, and Arabs came and occupied it."

We came to the asses' stalls. She said, "Do you see these stalls? Here stood a soup-kitchen, and the virtuous poor would enter in hungry and go forth satisfied. But they abandoned this place, and Arabs came and occupied it. Houses from which prayer and charity and study of the Torah never ceased, now belong to the Arabs and their asses. . . . My son, we have reached the courtyard of the *rabbanit*'s house. Go in, and I shall follow you later. This unhappy woman, because of the seeming good she has known abroad, does not see the true good at home."

"What is the true good?" I asked.

She laughed, saying, "My son, you should not need to ask. Have you not read the verse, 'Happy the man thou choosest to dwell in thy courtyards?' For these same courtyards are the royal courts of the Holy One, the courts of our God, in the midst of Jerusalem. When men say 'Jerusalem,' their way is to add the words, 'Holy City.' But when *I* say 'Jerusalem,' I add nothing more, since the holiness is contained in the name; yes, in the very name itself. . . . Go up, my son, and do not trip on the stairs. Many a time have I said to the keeper of the community funds that these stairs are in need of repair; and what answer did he give me? That this building is old and due to be demolished, therefore it is not worth while spending a penny on its upkeep. So the houses of Israel fall into disuse until they are

34

abandoned, and the sons of Ishmael enter and take possession. Houses that were built with the tears of their fathers—and now they abandon them. But again I have become a chatterer, and hasten my end."

I entered, and found the *rabbanit* lying in bed. Her head was bandaged and a poultice had been laid upon her throat. She coughed loudly, so that the medicine bottles placed by her bedside would shake at each cough. I said to her, *"Rabbanit,* are you ill?" She sighed and her eyes filled with tears. I sought for words of comfort, but the words would not come. All I could say, with my eyes downcast, was, "So you are ill and deserted."

She sighed again and replied, "Yes, I am ill as ill can be. In the whole world there is no one so ill as I am. All the same, I am not deserted. Even here in Jerusalem, where nobody knows me, and nobody knows the honors done to me in my own town, even here there is one woman who waits on me, who comes to my room and fetches a drop of soup for my royal feast. What do you hear from my grandson? He is angry with me, to be sure, because I have not written to thank him for the stove. Now I ask you, how shall I go out to buy ink and pen and paper for the writing of letters? It is hard enough even to fetch a spoonful of soup to my lips. . . . I am surprised that Tilli has not come."

"If you are speaking," said I, "of that gracious old woman who brought me here, she told me that she would come very soon."

"I cannot tell whether she is gracious," said the *rabbanit;* "at least she makes herself useful. Look you, how many holy, holy women there are about Jerusalem, who go buzzing like bees with their incantations and supplications, yet not one of them has come to me and said, *'Rabbanit,* do you need help?' . . . My head, my head.

If the pains in my heart won't take me off soon, the pains in my head will take me off first."

I said to her, "I can see that speech is a burden to you."

She answered, "You say that speech is a burden to me; and I say that my whole existence is a burden to me. Even the cat knows this, and keeps away from his home. Yet people say that cats are home-loving creatures. He finds my neighbor's mice more tasty, to be sure, than all the dainties I feed him. What was I meaning to say? I forget all I mean to say. Now Tilli is different. There she goes, with the bundles of years heaped up on her shoulders, bundle on bundle; yet all her wits serve her, although she must be twice my age. If my father—God bless his pious memory—were alive this day, he would be thought of as a child beside her."

I urged the *rabbanit* to tell me about this Tilli.

"And did you not mention her yourself? Nowadays people don't know Tilli; but there was a time when everyone did, for then she was a great, rich woman with all kinds of business concerns. And when she gave up all these and came to Jerusalem, she brought along with her I can't say how many barrels of gold, or if not barrels, there is no doubt that she brought a chest full of gold. My neighbors remember their mothers telling them how, when Tilli came to Jerusalem, all the best men here came courting, either for themselves or for their sons. But she sent them packing and stayed a widow. At first she was a very rich widow, and then a quite well-to-do widow, until at last she became just an old woman."

"Judging from Tilli's appearance," said I, "one would think that she had never seen hard times in her life."

The *rabbanit* replied with scorn, "You say that she has never seen hard times in her life, and I say that she has never seen good times in her life. There is no enemy of mine whom I would bless with the afflictions that Tilli has borne. You suppose that, because she is not reduced to living off the public funds, she has enjoyed a happy life, but I believe that there is not a beggar knocking on the doors who would exchange his sorrows for hers. . . . Oh, my aches and my pains. I try to forget them, but they will not forget me."

I perceived that the *rabbanit* knew more than she cared to disclose. Since I felt that no good would come of further questioning, I showed myself ready to leave by rising from my chair.

" 'The sweep hadn't stepped into the chimney, but his face was already black,' " said she. "You have scarcely sat down in your chair, and already you are up and away. Why all this haste?"

I said, "If you wish me to stay, I will stay."

She made no answer; so I began speaking of Tilli again, and asked if I might be told her story.

"And if I tell you," said the *rabbanit,* "will it benefit you, or benefit her? I have no liking for tale-bearers: they spin out their cobwebs, and call it fine tapestry. I will only say this, that the Lord did a mercy to that good man when He put the evil spirit into that apostate, may her name be blotted out. Why are you gaping at me? Don't you understand Yiddish?"

"I understand Yiddish quite well," said I, "but I cannot understand what you are saying, *rabbanit.* Who is the good man, and who is the apostate you have cursed?"

"Perhaps I should bless her then, perhaps I should say, 'Well done, Mistress Apostate, you who have changed the gold coin for the brass farthing.' See, again you are staring at me as if I were speaking Turkish. You have heard that my husband of blessed memory was a rabbi, wherefore they call me *rabbanit;* and have you not heard that my father too was a rabbi? Such a rabbi, that in comparison with him, all other rabbis might rank as pupils in a school for infants: and I speak of real rabbis, look you, not of those who wear the mantle and give themselves airs. . . . What a world, what a world it is! A deceitful world, and all it contains is deceit and vanity. But my father, of blessed and pious memory, was a rabbi from his childhood, and all the matchmakers in the province bustled about to find him a wife. Now there was a certain rich widow, and when I say rich, you know that I mean it. This widow had only one daughter—would she had never been born. She took a barrel full of gold dinars, and said to the matchmakers, 'If you wed that man to my daughter, this barrel full of gold will be his; and if it is not sufficient, I shall add to it!' But her daughter was not a fit match for that holy man; for she was already tainted with the spirit of perverseness, as is shown by her end, and she fled away from her home, and entered the house of the nuns, and deserted her faith. Yes, at the very hour when she was to be led to her bridal, she ran away. That poor stricken mother wasted half her fortune in trying to reclaim her. Her appeal went up to the Emperor himself; and even the Emperor was powerless to help. For they who have once entered the house of the nuns may never go out alive. You know now who that apostate was; the daughter of . . . hush, for here she comes."

Tilli entered the room. She was carrying a bowl of soup, and seeing me she said:

"Ah, you are still here! But stay, my friend, stay. It is a great *mitzvah* to visit the sick. *Rabbanit,* how much better you look! Truly, salvation comes in the wink of an eye; for the Name is healing you every minute. I have brought a little soup to moisten your lips, now, my dear, raise your head and I shall prop up your pillow. There, my dear, that's better. My son, I am sorry that you do not live in the City, for then you would see for yourself how the *rabbanit*'s health is improving day by day."

"And do I not live in Jerusalem?" I said. "Surely Nachlat Shivah is Jerusalem?"

"It is indeed," answered Tilli. "God forbid that it should be otherwise. Rather may the day come when Jerusalem extends as far as Damascus, and in every direction. But the eye that has seen all Jerusalem enclosed within her walls cannot accustom itself to viewing what is built beyond the walls as the City itself. It is true that all the Land of Israel is holy and, I need hardly say, the surroundings of Jerusalem: yet the holiness that is within the walls of the City surpasses all else. My son, there is nothing I have said which you do not know better than I. Why then have I said it? Only that I might speak the praise of Jerusalem."

I could read in the eyes of the *rabbanit* a certain resentment, because Tilli was speaking to me rather than to her. So I took my leave and went away.

Various preoccupations kept me for a while from going to the Old City; and after that came the nuisance of the tourists. How well we know these tourists, who descend upon us and upon the land, all because the Place has made a little space for us here! They come now to see what has happened; and having come, they regard us as if we were created solely to serve them. Yet one good thing may be said for the tourists: in showing them "the sights," we see them ourselves. Once or twice, having brought them to the City to show them the Wailing Wall, I met Tilli there. It seemed to me that a change had come over her. Although she had always walked without support, I noticed that she now leaned on a stick. Because of the visitors, I was unable to linger. For they had come to spy out the whole land, not to spend time upon an old woman not even mentioned in their itineraries.

When the tourists had left Jerusalem, I felt restless in myself. After trying without success to resume work, I bestirred myself and walked to the City, where I visited of my own accord all the places I had shown to the visitors. How can I describe what I saw? He who in his goodness daily renews the works of creation, perpetually renews his own City. New houses may not have been built, nor new trees planted, yet Jerusalem herself is ever new. I cannot explain the secret of her eternal variety. We must wait, all of us, for those great sages who will one day enlighten us.

I came upon that same man of learning whom I had visited earlier, and he drew me to his house, where he set before me all his recent findings. We sat together in deep contentment, while I asked my questions, and he replied; or spoke of problems, which he resolved; or mentioned obscure matters which he made clear. How good it is, how satisfying, to sit at the feet of one of the scholars of Jerusalem, and to learn the Law from his lips! His home is simple, his furnishings austere, yet his wisdom ranges far, like the great hill ranges of Jerusalem which are seen from the windows. Bare are the hills of Jerusalem; no temples or palaces crown them. Since the time of our exile, nation after nation has come and laid them waste. But the hills spread their glory like banners to the sky; they are resplendent in ever-changing hues; and not least in glory is the Mount of Olives, which bears no forest of trees, but a forest of tombs of the righteous, who in life and in death gave their thoughts to the Land.

As I stood up to go, the mistress of the house entered and said to her husband, "You have forgotten your promise." He was much perturbed at this, and said, "Wonder of wonders: all the time I have known Tehilah she has never asked a favor. And now she wants me to say that she wishes to see you."

"Are you speaking," said I, "of Tilli, the old woman who showed me the way to your house? For it seems to me that you call her by another name."

"Tehilah," he answered, "is Tilli's true name, that was given to her in the synagogue. From this you may learn that even four or five generations ago our forebears would give their daughters names that sound as though they had been recently coined. For this reason my wife's name is Tehiyah, or Reborn, which one might suppose to have been devised in our own age of rebirth. Yet in fact it belongs to the time of the great Gaon,* who required my wife's great-grandfather to call his daughter Tehiyah; and my wife bears her name."

I said, "You speak now of the custom four or five generations ago. Can it be that this Tehilah is so old?"

He smiled, saying, "Her years are not written upon her face, and she is not in the habit of telling her age. We only know it because of what she once let slip. It happened that Tehilah came to congratulate us at the wedding of our son; and the blessing she gave to our son and his bride was that it might be granted for them to live to her age. My son asked, 'What is this blessing with which you have blessed us?' And she answered him, 'It is ninety years since I was eleven years old.' This happened three years ago; so that now her age is, as she might express it, ninety years and fourteen: that is to say, a hundred and four."

I asked him, since he was already speaking of her,

* Literally, "genius," a title given to pre-eminent rabbinical scholars.

to tell me what manner of woman she was. He answered:

"What is there to say? She is a saint; yes, in the true meaning of the word. And if you have this opportunity of seeing her, you must take it. But I doubt if you will find her at home; for she is either visiting the sick, or bringing comforts to the poor, or doing some other unsolicited *mitzvah*. Yet you may perhaps find her, for between *mitzvah* and *mitzvah* she goes home to knit garments or stockings for poor orphans. In the days when she was rich, she spent her wealth upon deeds of charity, and now that nothing is left her but a meagre pittance to pay for her own few needs, she does her charities in person."

The scholar accompanied me as far as Tehilah's door. As we walked together he discoursed on his theories; but realizing that I was not attending to his words, he smiled and said, "From the moment I spoke of Tehilah, no other thought has entered your mind."

"I would beg to know more of her," I replied. He said:

"I have already spoken of her as she is today. How she was before she came to our land I do not know, beyond what everyone knows; that is to say, that she was a very wealthy woman, the owner of vast concerns, who gave up all when her sons and her husband died, and came here to Jerusalem. My late mother used to say, 'When I see Tehilah, I know that there is retribution worse than widowhood and the loss of sons.' What form of retribution this was, my mother never said; and neither I, nor anyone else alive, knows; for all that generation which knew Tehilah abroad is now dead, and she herself says but little. Even now, when she is beginning to change, and speaks more than she did, it is not of herself. . . . We have come to her house; but it is unlikely that you will find her at home; for towards sunset she makes the rounds of the schoolrooms, distributing sweets to the younger children."

A few moments later, however, I stood in the home of Tehilah. She was seated at the table, expecting me, so it seemed, with all her being. Her room was small, with the thick stone walls and arched ceiling that were universal in the Jerusalem of bygone days. Had it not been for the little bed in a corner, and a clay jar upon the table, I would have likened her room to a place of worship. Even its few ornaments—the hand-lamp of burnished copper, a copper pitcher and a lamp of the same metal that hung from the ceiling—even these, together with the look of the table, on which were laid a prayer-book, a Bible, and some third book of study, gave to the room the grace and simplicity of a house of prayer.

I bowed my head saying, "Blessed be my hostess."

She answered, "And blessed be my guest."

"You live here," said I, "like a princess."

"Every daughter of Israel," she said, "is a princess; and, praised be the living God, I too am a daughter of Israel. It is good that you have come. I asked to see you; and not only to see you, but to speak with you also. Would you consent to do me a favor?"

" 'Even to the half of my kingdom,' " I replied. She said:

"It is right that you should speak of your kingdom; for every man of Israel is the son of kings, and his deeds are royal deeds. When a man of Israel does good to his neighbor, this is a royal deed. Sit down, my son: it makes conversation more easy. Am I not intruding upon your time? You are a busy man, I am sure, and need the whole day for gaining your livelihood. Those times have gone when we had leisure enough and were glad to spend an hour in talk. Now everyone is in constant bustle and haste. People think that if they run fast enough it will speed the coming of Messiah. You see, my son, how I have become a chatterer. I have forgotten the advice of that old man who warned me not to waste words."

I was still waiting to learn the reason for her summons. But now, as if she had indeed taken to heart the old man's warning, she said nothing. After a while she glanced at me, and then looked away; then glanced at me again, as one might who is scrutinizing a messenger to decide if he is worthy of trust. At last she began to tell me of the death of the *rabbanit*, who had passed away during the night, while her stove was burning, and her cat lay warming itself at the flame—till the hearse-bearers came and carried her away, and someone unknown had taken the stove.

"You see, my son," said Tehilah, "a man performs a *mitzvah*, and one *mitzvah* begets another. Your deed was done for the sake of that poor woman, and now a second person is the gainer, who seeks to warm his bones against the cold." Again she looked me up and down; then she said, "I am sure you are surprised that I have troubled you to come."

"On the contrary," I said, "I am pleased."

"If you are pleased, so am I. But my pleasure is at finding a man who will do me a kindness; as for you, I do not know why you should be pleased."

For a moment she was silent. Then she said, "I have heard that you are skilful at handling a pen—since you are, as they nowadays call it, an author. So perhaps you will place your pen at my service for a short letter."

I took out my fountain pen. She looked at it with interest, and said, "You carry your pen about with you, like those who carry a spoon wherever they go, so that if they chance upon a meal, the spoon is ready to hand."

I replied, "For my part, I carry the meal inside the spoon." And I explained to her the working of my fountain pen.

She picked it up in her hand and objected, "You say there is ink inside, but I cannot see one drop."

I explained the principle more fully, and she said:

"If it is so, they slander your generation in saying that its inventions are only for evil. See, they have invented a portable stove, and invented this new kind of pen: it may happen that they will yet invent more things for the good of mankind. True it is that the longer one lives, the more one sees. All the same, take this quill that I have myself made ready, and dip it in this ink. It is not that I question the usefulness of your pen; but I would have my letter written in my own way. And here is a sheet of paper; it is crown-paper, which I have kept from days gone by, when they knew how good paper was made. Upwards of seventy years I have kept it by me, and still it is as good as new. . . . One thing more I would ask of you: I want you to write, not in the ordinary cursive hand, but in the capital letters of the prayer book and the Torah. I assume that as a writer you must at some time have transcribed, if not the Torah itself, at least the Scroll of Esther that we read on Purim.

"As a boy," I answered, "I copied such a scroll exactly in the manner prescribed; and, believe this or not, everyone who saw that scroll praised it."

"Although I have not seen it," said Tehilah, "I am sure you know how to write the characters as is required, without a single flaw. Now I shall make ready for you a glass of herb-tea, while you proceed with your writing."

"Please do not trouble," I said, "for I have already taken something to drink."

45

"If so, how shall I show hospitality? I know: I shall cut you a piece of sugar-loaf; then you can say a blessing, and I can add, Amen."

She gave me some of the sugar. Then, after a short silence, she said:

"Take up the quill and write. I shall speak in the vernacular, but you will write in the holy tongue. I have heard that now they teach the girls both to write and to speak the holy language: you see, my son, how the good Lord is constantly improving his world from age to age. When I was a child, this was not their way. But at least I understand my Hebrew prayer book, and can read from the Torah, and the Psalms, and the Ethics of the Fathers. . . . Oh dear, oh dear, today I have not finished my day."

I knew that she meant the day's portion of the Psalms, and said to her, "Instead of grieving you should rather be glad."

"Glad?"

"Yes," I said, "for the delay is from heaven, that one day more might be added to your sum of days." She sighed, and said:

"If I knew that tomorrow our Redeemer would come, gladly would I drag out another day in this world. But as day follows day, and still our true Redeemer tarries and comes not, what is my life? And what is my joy? God forbid that I should complain of my years: if it pleases Him to keep me in life, it pleases me also. Yet I cannot help but ask how much longer these bones must carry their burden. So many younger women have been privileged to set up their rest on the Mount of Olives, while I remain to walk on my feet, till I think I shall wear them away. And is it not better to present oneself in the Higher World while one's limbs are all whole, and return the loan of the body intact? I do not speak of putting on flesh, which is only an extra burden for the hearse-bearers. But at least it is good to die with whole limbs. . . . Again I am speaking too much: but now what does it matter a word less, or a word more. I am fully prepared to return the deposit of my body, earth back to earth. . . . Take up your quill, my son, and write."

I dipped the quill-pen in the ink, made ready the paper and waited for Tehilah to speak. But she was lost in her thoughts and seemed unaware of my presence. I sat there and gazed at her, my eyes taking in every wrinkle and furrow of her face. How many experiences she had known! She was in the habit of saying that she had seen good things, and yet better things. From what I had been told, these things seemed far from good. The adage was true of her, that the righteous wear mourning in their hearts, and joy upon their faces.

Tehilah became aware of me and, turning her head, said, "Have you begun?"

"You have not told me what I am to write."

She said, "The beginning does not need to be told. We commence by giving praise to God. Write: *With the help of the Holy Name, blessed be He.*"

I smoothed the paper, shook the quill, and wrote, *With the help of the Holy Name, blessed be He.*

She sat up, looked at what I had written, and said:

"Good; very good. And now what next? Write as follows: *From the Holy City, Jerusalem, may she be built and established, speedily and in our days, Amen.* In speech I only say 'Jerusalem,' without additions. But in writing, it is proper that we should bring to mind the holiness of Jerusalem, and add a plea for her to be rebuilt; that the reader may take Jerusalem to his heart, and know that she is in need of mercy, and say a prayer for her. Now, my son, write the day of the week, and

47

the portion of the Torah for the week, and the number of years since the creation."

When I had set down the full date, she continued:

"Now write, in a bold hand, and as carefully as you can, the letter *Lamed*. . . . Have you done this? Show me how it looks. . . . There is no denying that it is a good *Lamed*, though perhaps it could have been a trifle larger. Now, my son, continue with *Khaf*, and after the *Khaf* write *Bet*, and after it *Vav*. . . . *Vav*, I was saying, and now comes *Dalet*. Show me now the whole word, *Likhvod*, 'In honor of.' Very fine indeed. It is only right that the respectful address should be suitably written. Now add to that, *'the esteemed Rabbi'* . . . ah, you have already done so! You write faster than I think: while I am collecting my thoughts, you have already set them down. Truly your father—may the light of God shine on him—did not waste the cost of your education. . . . My son, forgive me, for I am so tired. Let us leave the writing of the letter till another day. When is it convenient for you to come?"

"Shall I come tomorrow?" I said.

"Tomorrow? Do you wish it? What day is tomorrow?"

"It is the day before new moon."

"That is a good day for this thing. Then let it be tomorrow."

I saw that she was inwardly grieved, and thought to myself: The day before new moon is a time for prayer and supplication, a time for visits to the tomb of Rachel our Mother; surely she will not be able to attend to her letter. Aloud I said to her, "If you are not free tomorrow I shall come on some other day."

"And why not tomorrow?"

"Just because it *is* the day before the new moon."

She said, "My son, you bring my sorrow before me,

48

that on such a day I should be unable to go to Rachel our Mother."

I asked why she could not go.

"Because my feet cannot carry me there."

"There are carriages," I said, "and buses as well."

"When I first came to Jerusalem," said Tehilah, "there were none of these buses, as they call them now, and a foolish word it is, too. There were not even carriages; so we used to walk. And since I have gone on foot for so long, it is now hardly worth changing my ways. Did you not say you are able to come tomorrow? If it pleases the Name to grant my wish, my life will be prolonged for yet a day more."

I left her and went on my way; and the following day I returned. I do not know if there was any real need to return so soon. Possibly if I had waited longer, it would have extended her life.

As soon as I saw her, I perceived a change. Tehilah's face, that always had about it a certain radiance, was doubly radiant. Her room shone out too. The stone floor was newly polished, and so were all the articles in the room. A white coverlet was spread over the little bed in the corner, and the skirtings of the walls were freshly color-washed blue. On the table stood the jar, with its parchment cover, and a lamp and sealing wax were placed at its side. When had she found time to color-wash the walls, and to clean the floor, and to polish all her utensils? Unless angels did her work, she must have toiled the night long.

She rose to welcome me, and said in a whisper, "I am glad that you have come. I was afraid you might forget, and I have a little business matter to attend to."

"If you have somewhere to go," I said, "I shall come back later."

"I have to go and confirm my lease. But since you

49

are here, sit down, and let us proceed with the letter. Then afterwards I shall go about my lease."

She set the paper before me and fetched the ink and the quill pen. I took up the pen and dipped it in the ink and waited for her to dictate her message.

"Are you ready?" she said. "Then I am ready too!"

As she spoke the word "ready," her face seemed to light up and a faint smile came to her lips. Again I prepared to write, and waited for her next words.

"Where did we leave off?" she said. "Was it not with the phrase, *In honor of the esteemed rabbi*? Now you shall write his name."

Still I sat waiting.

She said in a whisper, "His name is Shraga. . . . Have you written it?"

"I have written."

She half-closed her eyes as if dozing. After some time she raised herself from her chair to look at the letter, and whispered again, "His name is Shraga. His name is Shraga." And again she sat silent. Then she seemed to bestir herself, saying, "I shall tell you in a general way what you are to write." But again she lapsed back into silence, letting her eyelids droop.

"I see," she said at last, "that I shall have to tell you all that happened, so that you will understand these things and know how to write. It is an old story, of something which happened many years ago; yes, three and ninety years ago."

She reached for her walking stick and let her head sink down upon it. Then again she looked up, with an expression of surprise, as a man might who thinks he is sitting alone and discovers a stranger in his room. Her face was no longer calm, but showed grief and disquiet as she felt for her stick, then put it by, and again took it up to lean upon, passing her hand over her brow to smooth out her wrinkles.

Finally she said, "If I tell you the whole story, it will make it easier for you to write. . . . His name is Shraga. . . . Now I shall start from the very beginning."

She raised her eyes and peered about her; then, reassured that no one else could be listening, she began:

"I was eleven years old at the time. I know this, because Father, of blessed memory, used to write in his Bible the names of his children and the dates of their births, his daughters as well as his sons. You will find the names in that Bible you see before you; for when I came to Jerusalem, my late brothers renounced their right to my father's holy books and gave them to me. As I said before, it is an old story, three and ninety years old; yet I remember it well. I shall relate it to you, and little by little you will understand. Now, are you listening?"

I inclined my head and said, "Speak."

"So you see, I was eleven years old. One night, Father came home from the synagogue, bringing with him some relative of ours, and with them Petachya Mordechai, the father of Shraga. When she saw them enter, my dear mother—peace be upon her soul—called me and told me to wash my face well and put on my Sabbath dress. She too put on her Sabbath clothes and bound her silk kerchief round her head and, taking my hand, led me into the best room to meet Father and his guests. Shraga's father looked at me and said, 'Heaven shield you, you are a pretty child.' Father stroked my cheek and said, 'Tehilah, do you know who spoke to you? The father of your bridegroom-to-be spoke to you. May the influences be happy, my child: tonight you are betrothed.' At once all the visitors blessed me with happy influences, and called me 'the bride.' Mother quickly bundled me back to her room to shield me from any evil eye, and kissed me, and said, 'Now and henceforth, you are Shraga's betrothed; and God willing, next year, when your bridegroom comes of age at thirteen for wearing the phylacteries, we shall make your wedding.'

"I knew Shraga already, for we used to play with nuts and at hide-and-seek, until he grew too old and began to study the Gemara. After our betrothal I saw him every Sabbath, when he would come to Father's house and repeat to him all he had learned through the week. Mother would give me a dish of sweets which I would take and offer to Shraga, and Father would stroke my cheek and beam upon my bridegroom.

"And now they began to prepare for the wedding. Shraga's father wrote out the phylacteries, and my father bought him a prayer shawl, while I sewed a bag for the phylacteries and another bag for the prayer shawl that is worn on a Sabbath. Who made the large outer bag for both prayer shawl and phylacteries I cannot remember.

"One Sabbath, four full weeks before the day fixed for the wedding, Shraga failed to come to our house. During the afternoon service, Father enquired at the house of study, and was told that he had gone on a journey. Now this journey was made to one of the leaders of the Hasidim, and Shraga had been taken by his father in order that he might receive a direct blessing on the occasion of his first wearing of the prayer shawl and phylacteries. When my father learned this, his soul nearly parted from his body; for he had not known until then that Shraga's father was of the Sect. He had kept his beliefs a secret, for in those days the Hasidim were despised and persecuted, and Father was at the head of the persecutors; so that he looked upon members of the

Sect as if (God forbid) they had ceased to belong to our people. After the Havdalah ceremony at the close of the Sabbath, Father tore up my marriage contract and sent the pieces to the house of my intended father-in-law. On the Monday, Shraga returned with his father, and they came to our house. My father drove them out with abuse; whereupon Shraga himself swore an oath that he would never forgive us the insult. Now Father knew well that he who cancels a betrothal must seek pardon from the injured party; yet he took no steps to obtain this. And when my mother implored him to appease Shraga, he made light of her entreaties, saying, 'You have nothing to fear: he is only of the Sect.' So contemptible were the Hasidim in my father's eyes that he took no heed in this thing wherein all men take heed.

"Preparations for the wedding had been made. The poultry was ordered, and the house was cluttered with sacks of flour and casks of honey for the making of loaves and cakes. In short, all was ready, and there lacked nothing but a bridegroom. My father summoned a matchmaker; another bridegroom was found for me; and with him I went to my bridal.

"What became of Shraga, I do not know, for Father forbade any of our household to mention his name. Later I heard that he and all his people had moved to another town. Indeed they were in fear for their very lives, since, from the day when Father ended my betrothal, they were not called to the Law in synagogue—not even at the Rejoicing of the Law, when every man is called. They could not even come together for worship, for my father as head of the community would not let them assemble outside the fixed houses of prayer; and had they not moved to another town where they might be called to the Torah, they could not have gone through the year.

"Three years after the wedding, I was granted the birth of a son. And two years later, another son was born to me. And two years after that, I gave birth to a daughter.

"Time passed uneventfully, and we lived at our ease. The children grew and prospered, while I and my husband watched them grow and were glad. I forgot about Shraga, and forgot that I had never received a note of pardon at his hand.

"Mother and Father departed this life. Before his death, my father of blessed memory committed his affairs to his sons and his sons-in-law, enjoining them all to work together as one. Our business flourished, and we lived in high repute. We engaged good tutors for our sons, and a foreign governess for our daughter; for in those days pious folk would have nothing to do with the local teachers, who were suspected of being free-thinkers.

"My husband would bring these tutors from other towns; and whereas the local teachers were obliged to admit any student who came, even if he was not suitably qualified, tutors who had been brought from elsewhere were dependent upon those who engaged them and under no such obligation. Coming, as they did, alone, they would dine at our table on Sabbath days. Now my husband, who because of the pressure of his affairs could not make set times for study of the Torah, was especially glad of one such guest and his learned discourses. And I and the children delighted in the tuneful table chant he would sing us. We did not know that this tutor was a Hasid, and his discourses the doctrines of Hasidism, and the airs that he sang us, Hasidic airs; for in all other respects he conducted himself like any other true believer of Israel. One Sabbath eve, having discoursed of the Torah, he closed his eyes and sang a hymn of such heavenly bliss that our very souls went forth at its sweetness. At the end, my husband asked him, 'How may a man come to this experience of the divine?' The tutor whispered to him, 'Let your honor make a journey to my *rebbe*,* and he will know this and much more.'

"Some days later, my husband found himself in the city of the tutor's *rebbe*. On his return, he brought with him new customs, the like of which I had not seen in my father's house; and I perceived that these were the customs of the Hasidim. And I thought to myself, who can now wipe the dust from your eyes, Father, that you may see what you have done, you who banished Shraga for being a Hasid, and now the husband you gave me in his stead does exactly as he did? If this thing does not come about as atonement for sin, I know not why it has come about.

"My brothers and brothers-in-law saw what was happening, but they said not a word. For already the times had changed, and people were no longer ashamed to have Hasidim in the family. Men of wealth and position had come from other towns and married amongst us; they followed the customs of Hasidim, and even set up a house of prayer for their sect, and would travel openly to visit their *rebbes*. My husband did not attend their services, but in other respects he observed Hasidic customs and educated his sons in their ways, and from time to time would make journeys to his *rebbe*.

"A year before our first-born son came of age, there was plague in the world, and many fell sick. There was not a house without its victims, and when the plague reached us, it struck our son. In the end the Lord spared him—but not for long. When he rose from his sickbed,

* Yiddish for rabbi; usually applied to Hasidic leaders in Eastern Europe.

he began to study the practice of the phylacteries from the great code of the Shulhan Aruch. And I saw this and was glad, that for all his Hasidic training, his devotion to the Law was not lessened.

"One morning our son rose up very early to go to the house of study. As he was about to enter, he saw there a man dressed in grave clothes, resembling a corpse. It was not a dead man he had seen, but some demented creature who did many strange things. The child was overcome with terror and his senses left him. With difficulty was he restored to life. Restored to life he was indeed, but not to a long life. From that day on, his soul flickered and wavered like a candle flame, like the soul of a man at the closing prayer of the Day of Atonement, when his fate is about to be sealed. He had not come of age for wearing phylacteries when he gave up his ghost and died.

"Through the seven days of mourning I sat and meditated. My son had died after the Havdalah at the ending of Sabbath, thirty days before he came of age for phylacteries. And at the end of a Sabbath, after the Havdalah, thirty days before I was to go to my bridal with Shraga, Father had torn up the marriage contract. Counting the days I found to my horror that the two evils had come about on the same day, at the same hour. Even if this were no more than chance, yet it was a matter for serious reflection.

"Two years later, the boy's brother came of age— came, and did not come. He happened to go with his playfellows to the woods outside our town to fetch branches for the Pentecost. He left his comrades in the woods, intending to call on the scribe who was preparing his phylacteries; but he never returned. We thought at first that he had been stolen by gypsies, for a troop of them had been seen passing the town. After some days his body was found in the great marsh beside the woods; then we knew he must have missed his way and fallen in.

"When we stood up from our mourning, I said to my husband, 'Nothing remains to us now but our one daughter. If we do not seek forgiveness from Shraga, her fate will be as the fate of her brothers.'

"Throughout all those years we had heard nothing of Shraga. When he and his people left our town, they were forgotten, and their whereabouts remained unknown. My husband said, 'Shraga is the Hasid of such and such a *rebbe*: I shall make a journey to this man, and find out where he lives.'

"Now my husband was not the Hasid of this same *rebbe*: on the contrary, he was opposed to him, because of the great dispute that had broken out between the *rebbes,* on account of a cattle slaughterer, whom one had appointed and the other had dismissed. In the course of that quarrel a man of Israel was killed, and several families were uprooted, and several owners of property lost their possessions, and several persons ended their days in prison.

"Nevertheless, my husband made the journey to the town where this *rebbe* lived. Before he arrived there, the *rebbe* died, after dividing his ministry amongst his sons, who went away each to a different town. My husband journeyed from town to town, from son to son, inquiring of each son where Shraga might be. Finally he was told, 'If you are asking after Shraga, Shraga has become a renegade and joined our opponents.' But no one knew where Shraga now lived.

"When a man is a Hasid, you may trace him without difficulty. If he is not the disciple of one *rebbe,* he is the disciple of another. But with any ordinary un-attached Jew, unless you know where he lives, how may he be found? My husband, peace be upon his soul, was accustomed to making journeys, for his business took him to many places. He made journey after journey inquiring for Shraga. On account of these travels his strength in time began to fail and his blood grew thin. At last, having traveled to a certain place, he fell sick there and died.

"After I had set up his tombstone, I went back to my town and entered into business. While my husband was still alive, I had helped him in his affairs: now that he was dead, I speeded them with all my might. And the Lord doubled my powers until it was said of me, 'She has the strength of a man.' It would have been well, perhaps, had wisdom been granted me in place of strength, but the Lord knows what he intends and does not require his own creatures to tell him what is good. I thought in my heart: all this toil is for my daughter's sake. If I add to my wealth, I shall add to her welfare. As my responsibilities became ever greater, I found I had no leisure to spend at home, except on Sabbaths and holy days, and even these days were apportioned, half to the service in synagogue, and the other half to the reception of guests. My daughter, so it seemed, was in no need of my company, for I had engaged governesses, and she was devoted to her studies. I received much praise on account of my daughter, and even the gentiles, who deride our accent, would say that she spoke their language as well as the best of their people. Furthermore, these governesses would ingratiate themselves with my daughter, and invite her to their homes. In due course, I called the matchmakers, who found her a husband distinguished for his learning, and already qualified for the rabbinate. But I was not to enjoy a parent's privilege of leading my daughter to her bridal, for the evil spirit took possession of her, so that her right reason was perverted.

"And now, my son, this is what I ask of you: Write to Shraga for me, and say that I have forgiven him for all the sorrows that befell me at his hand. And say that I think he should forgive me, too, for I have been stricken enough."

For a long, long time I sat in silence, unable to speak a word. At last, secretly wiping a tear from my eye, I said to Tehilah:

"Allow me to ask a question. Since the day when your father tore up the marriage contract, ninety years and more have passed. Do you really believe that Shraga is still alive? And if so, has anyone informed you where he may be found?"

Tehilah answered, "Shraga is not alive. Shraga has now been dead for thirty years. I know the year of his death, for in that year, on the seventh day of Adar, I went to a synagogue for the afternoon service. Following the week's reading from the Prophets, they said the memorial prayer for the dead, and I heard them pray for the soul of Shraga. After the service, I spoke to the beadle of the synagogue, and asked him who this Shraga might be. He mentioned the name of a certain kinsman of the dead man, who had given instructions for his soul to be remembered. I went to this kinsman, and heard what I heard."

"If Shraga is dead, then, how do you propose to send him a letter?"

Tehilah answered, "I suppose you are thinking that this old woman's wits are beginning to fail her, after so many years; and that she is relying upon the post office to deliver a letter to a dead man."

I said, "Then tell me, what will you do?"

She rose, and picking up the clay jar that stood on the table, raised it high above her head, intoning in a kind of ritual chant:

"I shall take this letter—and set it in this jar; I shall take this wax—and seal up this jar; and I shall take them with me—this letter and this jar."

I thought to myself, and even if you take the jar and the letter with you, I still do not see how your message will come to Shraga. Aloud I said to her, "Where will you take your jar with its letter?"

Tehilah smiled and said softly, "Where will I take it? I will take it to the grave, my son. Yes, I shall take this jar, and the letter inside it, straight to my grave. For up in the High World they know Shraga well and will know where to find him. And the postmen of the Holy One are dependable, you may be sure; they will see that the letter is delivered."

Tehilah smiled again. It was a little smile of triumph, as of a precocious child who has got the better of an argument with her elders. After a while she let her head sink upon her walking stick and seemed again to be half asleep. But soon she glanced up and said, "Now that you understand the whole matter, you can write of your own accord." And again her head dropped over her stick.

I took up the pen and wrote the letter. When I had finished, Tehilah raised her head and inquired, "Is it done now?" I began to read the letter aloud, while she sat with her eyes closed, as if she had lost interest in the whole matter and no longer desired very greatly to hear. When the reading was over, she opened her eyes and said:

"Good, my son, good and to the point. Perhaps it might have been phrased rather differently, but even so, the meaning is clear. Now, my son, hand me the pen and I shall sign my name. Then I can put the letter in the jar; and after that I shall go about my lease."

I dipped the pen in the ink and handed it to her, and

she took it and signed her name. She passed the pen over certain of the characters to make them more clear. Then she folded the letter and placed it inside the jar, and bound the piece of parchment over the top. Then she kindled the lamp, and took wax for sealing, and held it against the flame until the wax became soft; then she sealed the jar with the wax. Having done these things, she rose from her place and went towards her bed. She lifted up the coverlet and placed the jar under the pillow of the bed. Then she looked at me fairly, and said in a quiet voice:

"I must make haste to confirm my lease. Bless you, my son, for the pains you have taken. Now and henceforth I shall not trouble you more."

So saying, she made smooth the coverlet of her bed, and took up her stick, and went to the door, and reached up that she might lay her lips to the mezuzah, and waited for me to follow. She locked the door behind us and walked ahead with brisk steps; and I overtook her and continued at her side.

As she walked, she looked kindly upon every place that she passed and every person she met. Suddenly she stopped and said, "My son, how can they abandon these holy places and these faithful Jews?"

At that time, I still did not comprehend all she meant by these words. When we reached the parting of the ways, she stopped again and said, "Peace with you." But when she saw that I was resolved not to leave her, she said no more. She went up the wide steps that lead to the courtyard of the Communal Center, and entered, and I followed.

We went into the Communal Center, which administers the affairs of the living and the dead. Two of the clerks sat there at a desk, their ledgers before them and their pens in their hands, writing and taking sips of their

Turkish coffee as they wrote. When they saw Tehilah, they set down their pens and stood up in respect. They spoke their welcome, and hastened to bring her a chair.

"What brings you here?" asked the elder of the clerks.

She answered, "I have come to confirm my lease."

He said, "You have come to confirm your lease: and we are of opinion that the time has come to annul it."

Tehilah was amazed. "What is all this?" she cried.

He said, "Surely you have already joined the immortals?"

Laughing at his own joke, the clerk turned to me, saying, "Tehilah, bless her, and may she live for many, many years, is in the habit of coming every year to confirm the bill of sale on the plot for her grave on the Mount of Olives. So it was last year, and the year before that, and three years ago, and ten and twenty and thirty years ago, and so will she go on till the coming of the Redeemer."

Said Tehilah, "May he come, the Redeemer: may he come, the Redeemer. Would to God he would hasten and come. But as for me, I shall trouble you no more."

The clerk asked, assuming a tone of surprise, "Are you going to a kibbutz, then, like these young girls they call 'pioneers'?"

Tehilah said, "I am not going to a kibbutz, I am going to my own place."

"What, said the clerk, "are you returning to your home country?"

Tehilah said, "I am not returning to my home country, but I am returning to the place whence I came: as it is written, *'And to the dust thou shalt return.'*"

"Tut-tut," said the clerk, "do you think that the Burial Society has nothing to do? Take my advice, and wait for twenty or thirty years more. Why all this haste?"

She said quietly, "I have already ordered the corpse-washers and the layers-out, and it would be ill-mannered to make sport of these good women."

The clerk's expression changed, and it was evident that he regretted his light words. He then said:

"It is good for us to see you here, for so long as we see you, we have before us the example of a long life; and should you desert us—God forbid—it is as if you take away from us this precedent."

Tehilah said, "Had I more years to live, I would give them gladly to you, and to all who delight in life. Here is the lease for you to sign."

When the clerk had endorsed the bill of sale, Tehilah took it and placed it in the fold of her dress.

"Now and henceforth I shall trouble you no more," she said. "May the Name be with you, dear countrymen; for I go to my place."

She rose from her chair, and walked to the door and reached up to lay her lips to the mezuzah, and kissed the mezuzah, and so went away.

When she saw that I still went with her, she said, "Return to your own life, my son."

"I thought," said I, "that when you spoke of confirming the lease, you meant the lease of your house; but instead . . ."

She took me up in the midst of my words. "But instead," said she, "I confirmed the lease of my long home. Yet may the Holy One grant that I have no need to dwell there for long, before I rise again, with all the dead of Israel. Peace be upon you, my son. I must make haste and return to my house, for I am sure that the corpse-washers and the layers-out already await me."

I stood there in silence and watched her go, until she passed out of sight among the courts and the alleys.

Next morning I went to the Old City to enquire how

she fared. On my way, I was stopped by the man of learning to whose house Tehilah had led me. For some while he kept me in conversation, and when I wished to take my leave, he offered to accompany me.

"I am not going home yet," I said. "I am going to see Tehilah."

He said, "Go only after a hundred and twenty years."

Seeing my surprise, he added, "You will live. But that saint has now left us."

I parted from him and went on alone. As I walked, I thought again and again: Tehilah has left us, she has gone on alone; she has left us, and gone on alone. I found that my feet had carried me to the house of Tehilah, and I opened her door and entered.

Still and calm was the room, like a house of prayer after the prayer has been said. There, on the stone floor, flowed the last tiny rivulets of the waters in which Tehilah had been cleansed.

—Translated by Walter Lever

HAIM HAZAZ

The
Sermon

*Haim Hazaz was born in the
Ukraine in 1898 and has
lived in Israel since 1931.
He began to write in the
nineteen-twenties while in
Constantinople and Paris,
during the course of a pro-
tracted emigration from post-
war Russia to Palestine, and
has published prolifically
since then. His works include
three novels (an English
translation of one appeared
in 1956 under the title* Mori
Said); *a tetralogy; a four-act
play; and numerous short
stories.*

*Hazaz's choice of subject
matter has been far-ranging,
extending from reminiscences
of his native Ukrainian Jewry
to the life of the Yemenite
Jews in Israel, a community
in which he has taken a special interest. "The Sermon"
is essentially a soliloquy on
the nature of Jewish history,
but the setting for this—a
meeting of the central committee of a kibbutz or communal farm—provides the
story with an added satirical
dimension.*

Yudka was no speaker. He didn't make public addresses, never took part in the debate at general meetings or at conventions—not even to make a point of order. So he was considered a man whose strength was not in self-expression. And, even though he was not just as he was considered to be, his reputation had its effect; it became second nature to him, so that he quite forgot how to open his mouth in public and say something in proper form, whether it was important or no more than a jest. That was why the boys were astounded when they heard he proposed to deliver a formal statement before the committee; and the committee, whose proceedings were open only to its members and to individuals called in before it, was convened at that time for no other reason than to hear him speak.

The committee members sat in a single row at the green table, right and left of their chairman, all clean-cut and positive, like captains and heroes in council. They eyed Yudka curiously, waiting to hear him say something not yet heard or known, except the chairman, who gazed straight at the table, apparently dreaming or drowsing, with cool eyes.

The chairman dutifully spoke a few words of introduction, fell silent, and sat down, just as though he hadn't opened his mouth, and there were no one else in the room.

Yudka drew himself up stiffly, looking harried and confused, so much did he have to say and so little did he know how to begin.

It was shocking, how confused and how harried he was! This quarryman, who split rocks and rent mountains, and went out fearlessly on night patrols, no sooner had to speak publicly before his comrades, than he lost himself completely from fright.

They waited, and he said nothing. Again the chairman spoke, directly to the green-covered table: "Comrade Yudka has the floor."

Yudka stood there crumbling inwardly, drops of sweat glistening on his brow.

"You wanted to make a statement," the chairman prompted, glancing slantwise at him, "Well then, speak. We're listening."

Some of the committee members looked aside, some stared off into space; all were silent.

At last Yudka passed his hand over his forehead, and said in the soft, slurred accent of the South of Russia: "I didn't come here to make a speech, only to say something important. . . . Really, I shouldn't say anything at all. . . . Do you know what it is to speak when it's best for you to keep still?"

He looked down the line of seats, parting his lips in an injured smile, faint and sickly.

"But I must speak!" He fixed his eyes in a blank stare, his face clouding. "I don't understand anything at all . . . I no longer understand. It's been years since I've understood. . . ."

"What don't you understand?" the chairman asked him calmly, like a judge trained to be patient with the public.

"Everything!" Yudka called out with passion. "Everything! But that's nonsense. Let's leave that for now. All I want to know is: What are we doing here?"

"Doing where?" The chairman did not follow him.

"Here! In this place, or in Palestine. In general. . . ."

"*I* don't understand!" The chairman spread his hands wonderingly, and his lips twisted in a mocking smile. "Now *I* don't understand either. . . ."

"That's a different way of not understanding," Yudka rejoined. "That's probably your way of mocking me."

One of the committee members broke into a broad

grin and tapped his fingers on the table top. Yudka felt his smile, but lowered his eyes, pretending not to see.

"Get back to the subject!" the chairman demanded. "Make the statement you want to make, without argument."

"I want to state," Yudka spoke with an effort, in low, tense tones, "that I am opposed to Jewish history. . . ."

"What?" The chairman looked about him to either side.

The committee members exchanged glances in astonishment. The one who had smiled at first could no longer control himself, and a short explosive laugh escaped him.

"I have no respect for Jewish history!" Yudka repeated the same refrain. " 'Respect' is really not the word, but what I said before: I'm opposed to it. . . ."

Once again the same comrade—a lively fellow by nature—burst into laughter and all the others joined in.

Yudka turned and looked at him.

"You're laughing," he said in a voice dulled and measured and serious beyond words, "because you took my wife from me. . . ."

At once they all fell silent and shrank back, as if from some imminent danger, and the comrade who had laughed was thrown into confusion. Shifting and slouching, he sat with bowed back and restless eyes.

The chairman struck four or five strokes with all his might on the bell, and then again three more from sheer shock and helplessness, with no idea of what to say.

"I think that's how it is," Yudka went on, after the ringing had ceased. "If I were in his place, I would laugh too every time I saw him . . . not straight in his face, but like that . . . it's a different kind of laugh! I couldn't help laughing, I wouldn't dare . . . I couldn't manage to do anything else or say anything . . . for I would feel terribly ashamed then . . . terribly ashamed! I couldn't talk to him freely, for example, let's say about literature. Or perhaps make my confession and weep . . . I can't explain it very well, but it's clear! I've thought it all out and made sure that that's how it is. But it's not important. . . ."

For a while there was quiet, a total, final quiet in the room.

Then the chairman stirred, beetling his heavy eyebrows, and spoke with gruff, ironical severity: "Comrade Yudka, I call you to order! If you have something to say, please, say it briefly, no wandering off the subject. And if it's history you want to talk about, then the university is the place for you!"

"It's on the subject, it's on the subject!" Yudka hastened to reply with a propitiating smile. "I can't proceed now without history. I've thought a great deal about it, many nights, every night when I'm on guard. . . ."

The chairman shrugged and spread his hands skeptically. "Speak!" he ordered, to cut it short.

Yudka became as before: confused and harried, as though at that very moment some ill fortune had befallen him and he had come to pain and torment.

"You've already heard that I'm opposed to Jewish history." He coughed in shame and unease, as he began the sermon. "I want to explain why. Just be patient a little while. . . . First, I will begin with the fact that we have no history at all. That's a fact. And that's the *zagvozdka*. I don't know how to say it in Hebrew. . . . In other words, that's where the shoe pinches. Because we didn't make our own history, the *goyim* made it for us. Just as they used to put out our candles on Sabbath, milk our cows and light our ovens on Sabbath, so they made our history for us to suit themselves, and we took it from them as it came. But it's not ours, it's not ours at all! Because we didn't make it, we would have made it differently, we didn't want it to be like that, it was only others who wanted it that way and they forced it on us, whether we liked it or not, which is a different thing altogether. . . . In that sense, and in every other sense, I tell you, in every other sense, we have no history of our own. Have we? It's clear as can be! And that's why I'm opposed to it, I don't recognize it, it doesn't exist for me! What's more, I don't respect it, although 'respect' is not the word, still I don't respect it . . . I don't respect it at all! But the main thing is, I'm opposed to it. What I mean is, I don't accept it. . . ."

The storm within him made him shake from side to side like an ox refusing the yoke. He swung his hands about as if he were moving stone or sorting lumber, and he was so swept along in his speech that he could no longer halt.

"I don't accept it!" he repeated, with the stubborn insistence of one who has come to a final, fixed opinion. "Not a single point, not a line, not a dot. Nothing, nothing . . . nothing at all! Will you believe me? Will you believe me? You can't even imagine how I'm opposed to it, how I reject it, and how . . . how . . . I don't respect it! Now, look! Just think . . . what is there in it? Just give me an answer: What is there in it? Oppression, defamation, persecution, martyrdom. And again oppression, defamation, persecution, and martyrdom. And again and again and again, without end. . . . That's what's in it, and nothing more! After all, it's . . . it's . . . it bores you to death, it's just plain dull! Just let me mention one fact, just one little fact. It's well known that children everywhere love to read historical fiction. That's where you get action, see, bold deeds, heroes, great fighters, and fearless conquerors. In a word, a world full of heroism. Now, here now, in Palestine, our children love to read, unless they're stupid. I know this for a fact. I've looked into it. Yes, they read, but historical novels about *goyim,* not about Jews. Why is that so? It's no accident. It's simply because Jewish history is dull, uninteresting. It has no glory or action, no heroes and conquerors, no rulers and masters of their fate, just a collection of wounded, hunted, groaning, and wailing wretches, always begging for mercy. You can see for yourselves that it can't be interesting. The least you can say is it's uninteresting. I would simply forbid teaching our children Jewish history. Why the devil teach them about their ancestors' shame? I would just say to them: 'Boys, from the day we were driven out from our land we've been a people without a history. Class dismissed. Go out and play football. . . .' But that's all in passing. So, let me proceed. I'm sure you won't take me wrong. I know that there is heroism in the way we stood up to all that oppression and suffering. I take it into account. . . . But . . . I don't care for that kind of heroism. Don't laugh . . . I don't care for it! I prefer an entirely different kind of heroism. First of all, please understand me, it's nothing but the heroism of despair. With no way out, anyone can be a hero. Whether he wants to or not, he must be, and there is no credit or honor in that. In the second place, this heroism after all amounts to great weakness, worse than weakness, a kind of special talent for corruption and decay. That's how it is! This type of hero sooner or later begins to pride himself on his 'heroism' and brags about it: 'See what great torments I withstand! See what untold shame and humiliation I suffer! Who can compare with me? See, we don't merely suffer torments. It's more than that, we love these torments too, we love torment for its own sake. . . . We

want to be tortured, we are eager, we yearn for it. . . .
Persecution preserves us, keeps us alive. Without it, we
couldn't exist. . . . Did you ever see a community of
Jews that was not suffering? I've never seen one. A Jew
without suffering is an abnormal creature, hardly a
Jew at all, half a *goy*. . . . That's what I mean; it's just
such 'heroism' that shows our weakness . . . suffering,
suffering, suffering! Everything is rotten around suffering. . . . Please notice, I said *around,* not *in* suffering.
There's a tremendous difference. . . . Everything,
everything around it rots: history, life itself, all actions,
customs, the group, the individual, literature, culture,
folk songs . . . everything! The world grows narrow,
cramped, upside down. A world of darkness, perversion
and contradiction. Sorrow is priced higher than joy,
pain easier to understand than happiness, wrecking
better than building, slavery preferred to redemption,
dream before reality, hope more than the future, faith
before common sense, and so on for all the other per-
versions . . . It's horrible! A new psychology is created, a kind of *moonlight* psychology. . . . The night
has its own special psychology, quite different from the
day's. I don't mean the psychology of a man at night,
that's something separate, but the psychology of night
itself. You may not have noticed it, perhaps, but it's
there, it's there. I know it. I feel it every time I stand
guard. The whole world behaves quite differently too
in the day, nature moves in a different way, every blade
of grass, every stone, every smell, all different, different. . . ."

"Yudka," the chairman cut in, half jesting, half be-
seeching, "your thoughts are very fine, but have pity on
us. Why did you have the committee convened?"

"Wait, wait," said Yudka hastily, "I haven't come to
the main thing. You don't know yet . . . I have some-

thing in mind, I have something in mind. . . . You'll soon see. Just be patient a little . . ."

"Let him talk," spoke up one of the committee, "let him talk."

"But . . ." the chairman began dubiously.

At that moment Yudka unintentionally shouted at him: "Quiet!" The chairman was cowed and submitted in silence.

"I'm not wandering from the subject. I'm speaking about principles, about basic things. . . ." Yudka fumbled wide-eyed, his earnestness written on his face, his mind obviously entangled and exalted, laboring and driving toward something.

In a short while, he began again:

"I've already told you, and I beg you to remember that a special, perverted, fantastic psychology has grown up among us, if I may say so, a *moonlight* psychology, altogether different in every way from other people's. . . . We love suffering, for through suffering we are able to be Jews; it preserves us and maintains us, it proves we are bold and heroic, braver than any people in the whole world. I admit, I am forced to admit that this is heroic indeed, in a way. People, you know, abuse many fine and noble words . . . in a certain sense suffering is heroic. And in a sense even decay is heroic and degradation is heroic . . . that is exactly the kind of people we are. We don't fight, or conquer, or rule. We have no desire, no will for it. Rather, we submit, we suffer without limit, willingly, lovingly. We actually say: You shall not conquer us, nor break us, nor destroy us! There is no power on earth strong enough for that . . . because power has its limits, but there is no limit, no end to our suffering. . . . In fact, the more we are oppressed, the greater we grow; the more we are degraded, the greater we think is our honor; the more we

are made to suffer, the stronger we become. For this is
our staple food, it is our elixir of life. . . . It's all so
beautifully arranged! A character like that, imagine it,
a nature so perfected . . . and that explains everything: Exile, martyrdom, Messiah . . . these are three
which are one, all to the same purpose, the same intention. . . . Doesn't it say somewhere: 'The threefold
cord'? . . ."

" 'And the threefold cord is not quickly broken,' "
contributed one of the committee.

"That's it!" Yudka seized upon the verse excitedly.
"Not quickly broken! Not quickly! Never, never. . . .
These three support each other, aid and abet each other,
so that never will the Jews be redeemed in all the world
. . . so that they wander from nation to nation and
country to country, age upon age to the end of all ages,
the weight of the laws falling upon them, the fury of the
lawless rising against them, everywhere trials and tribu-
lations and foes and hatred on every hand. . . . Exile,
exile . . . Oh oh, how they love it, how they hold it
fast! This is the most sacred thing, the most beloved,
intimate, closest to their hearts, nearer and dearer than
Jerusalem, more *Jewish* than Jerusalem, deeper and
purer. Far more, there's simply no comparison! Is this
a paradox? But that's how it is. . . . Wait now, don't
talk!" He hurriedly gestured to each side, though nobody
made any attempt to interrupt. "Let me tell you how I
look at it. . . ."

He rubbed his hand over his face and lips, as though
coming up out of a tub; he muted his voice and whispered, as though it were a deep secret.

"The Exile, that is our pyramid, and it has martyrdom for a base and Messiah for its peak. And . . .
and . . . the Talmud, that is our Book of the Dead.
. . . In the very beginning, as far back as the Second

Temple, we began to build it. Even that far back we planned it, we laid the foundations. . . . Exile, martyrdom, Messiah. . . . Do you grasp the deep cunning hidden in this wild fantasy, the cold *moonlight* with which it flames . . . ? Do you grasp it? Just think, just think! Millions of men, a whole people plunging itself into this madness and sunk in it for two thousand years! Giving up to it its life, its very existence, its character, submitting to affliction, suffering, tortures. Agreed that it is foolish, a lunatic dream. But a dream, that is, a vision, an ideal. . . . What an uncanny folk! What a wonderful, awful people! Awful, awful to the point of madness! For look, it scorns the whole world, the whole world and all its fighters and heroes and wise men and poets all together! Fearsome and blind! A bottomless abyss. . . . No, one could go mad!"

He formed the last words soundlessly on his lips and stood as though in trance, pale, with his mouth open and a fixed stare.

The chairman invited him to be seated. "Sit down," he said, pointing to an empty chair.

"What?" He came to himself, speaking as out of a maze. "But it's not just a fantasy, it's more than fantasy . . . fantastic, to be sure. But a necessary fantasy. . . . Why necessary? What is its purpose? A very necessary purpose, let me tell you, a vitally necessary purpose! This madness is practical, it is very deliberate, it has a clearly understood aim, and it is thought out to the finest detail. . . . Look here, here we have a single element, as slight as can be, a trifling anecdote, with consequences as grave, as far-reaching as can be . . . I'm speaking of the belief in the Messiah. That's a typical Jewish fantasy, the most typical of all! Isn't it? . . . A single myth, all that is left of the whole past, the closing speech of all that great drama, after the Judges, the Prophets, and the Kings, after the First Temple and the Second, after the wars and wonders—well, and all the rest of it. . . . And that's what we are left with—a single, simple legend, and no more. Not much, you say? You are mistaken. On the contrary, it is a great deal. It is far too much. You might think, it's no more than a trifle, a kindergarten legend. But it's not so. It's by no means so innocent. It has such a cunning, do you know, like that of well-tried, ancient men, a cunning of the greatest subtlety, so fated, so *podlaya*—that is, so corrupt a cunning. . . . Let me add, by the way, it's a wonderful legend, a tale of genius, although—apart from the philosophy and symbolism in it—not free of caricature, you know, not without a biting Jewish wit and humor; he comes on an ass! A great, a colossal, a cosmic image —not on a snorting steed, but precisely on a donkey, on the most miserable and insignificant of animals. . . . And this was enough to determine a people's fate and chart its course in the world for endless ages, for all eternity, this, and not the disputes of the schools of Shammai and Hillel. I'm not familiar with these things, I never learned Talmud, but it's quite clear. . . . It's an obvious thing, a certainty that if not for this myth it would all have been different. For then, they would finally have had to go right back to Palestine or somehow or other pass on out of the world. At any rate, they would have had to think of something or do something, somehow or other, to bring it all to an end. . . ."

Once more the chairman thought of making him bring his speech to an end, for it seemed to him that the whole discussion was out of place in the committee. He turned to both sides, consulting the committee members with a glance: "What do you think?" They signed to him to let him go on. He acquiesced and settled back.

Yudka did not notice the exchange of signals at all,

but went on: "Now there is no need. Now they needn't think about anything or do anything, not a single thought or the slightest action. King Messiah will do it all for them, and they have nothing to do but sit and wait for his coming. In fact, it's forbidden to get involved in the whole matter, to force the end. Forbidden! What can this thing mean?" His voice shook. "What can it mean? . . . Under orders, under orders to stay in Exile until in *Heaven* they decide to redeem them. Not by their own will or their own acts, but from Heaven; not in the way of nature, but by wonders and miracles . . . you understand?"

His eyes passed down the seated line, and he stood there marveling, momentarily struck dumb.

"Do you understand?" he repeated, out of wonder and oppression of mind. "They do nothing, not an effort, nothing at all, just sit and wait. . . . They invented a Messiah in Heaven, but not as a legend out of the past, as a promise for their future. That's very important, terribly important—and they trust in him to come and bring their redemption, while they themselves are obliged to do nothing at all and there you have it. . . . How can they believe in such a thing! And so to believe! To believe for two thousand years! Two thousand years! . . . How, how can men who are by no means simple, who are no fools at all, on the contrary, very shrewd men, men with more than a touch of skepticism, men who are practical, and maybe even a bit too practical, how can they believe something like that, *a thing like that*—and not just believe, but trust in it, pin their whole life upon it, the whole substance of their life and survival, their national, historic fate? . . . And quite seriously, in full earnest! For truly they believe with perfect faith . . . the whole thing is that they really believe! And yet, and yet, in the secrecy of their hearts,

77

you know, deep down, in some hidden fold, some geometric point down there in their hearts—*somewhat* they don't believe, just the faintest hint; at any rate, that he will come now, at this very moment, that he will come during their own lives, in their day, and this, of course, is the core of the matter. . . . It would not be possible for them not to *not* believe, even though, generally speaking, they believe with perfect faith! See? . . . This is a Jewish trait too, a very Jewish trait: to believe with perfect faith, with the mad and burning faith of all the heart and all the soul, and yet *somewhat* not to believe, the least little bit, and to let this tiny bit be decisive . . . I can't explain it well. But that's how it is. I am not mistaken! How complicated it all is! . . . Redemption is the chief of all their desires, the whole substance of their hopes, and yet they have bound themselves, locked their hands and feet in chains, and sealed their own doom, guarding and observing their own sentence with unimaginable pedantic strictness, not to be redeemed for ever and ever! Well, now then . . . now then . . . the birth pangs of Messiah. . . . That's an entire, separate chapter, a very interesting chapter. . . . Why must there be, according to the folk belief, why must a time of great troubles come before the end of days? What for? . . . Why couldn't they do without the troubles? After all, he is Messiah and he has unlimited power. . . . Why couldn't he come amid joy, with goodness and blessings, in the midst of peace? . . . And look: It's not troubles for Israel's enemies particularly, for the gentiles, but especially for Israel! Nor are these troubles such, let's say, that would make them repent and so on, but just troubles for the sake of trouble, with no rhyme or reason, a whole flood of troubles, plagues, and oppressions and every kind of torment, until the eyes of Israel grow weary with beholding the grief and agony, till they can no longer bear it, and they despair of redemption. . . . What is this? A *Weltanschauung?* Historic wisdom? Or is it perhaps what one dare not hint: simply their own fear of redemption? . . . I am just lost!"

He really looked lost, standing there. He seemed for a moment to have forgotten himself completely, and not to know where he was.

"It seems to me," he said, with a vague, sickly smile, "I once heard there was a sage or a pious man, I forget which, who said it already: 'Let him come, and may I not see it,' or something like that. . . . Maybe it was a joke, a cynical remark, or just chatter. Or maybe it was a great truth, revealing a secret deep, deep buried. . . . How was this myth ever invented at all? Not invented, no . . . I don't mean to say that . . . because in the beginning surely there was nothing but hope and longing for the kingdom of the House of David. . . . But how did it become what it turned into afterwards, the classic creation of the people, one might say the creation of its highest genius, the eternal creation of the people of Israel? What made it, more than any other myth, sink so deep and spread so wide in the folk-mind that it became common to everyone, rabbis and thinkers and the mass of people, scholars and illiterates, man, woman and child? What was there in it to let it dye our very heart's blood, and rise to a kind of dogma of faith and religion, the foundation of the whole people's life for all ages, our national idea, our vision in history, our political program, and so on? Whatever the answer— it did! That's the fact. It means there must be a profound kinship, a fundamental bond between this myth and the spirit of our people, if it thrust so deep! It means there is a basic harmony, a full and perfect unity between it and our people's ideal, between it and the people's will, and the direction it desires to go! . . . There's not the least doubt: it's quite clear!"

He stopped for a moment, and his face turned dull and pale. It was quiet in the room, as quiet as in the season just before the rains come, a waiting, oppressive, gloomy quiet.

"Ye-es . . ." he said with a long, groaning breath, as if speaking from his very heart, "such is that wild, enthusiastic, *moonlit* fantasy of theirs . . . the fantasy they need for such practical purposes, for their well-understood ends. Just as I've already told you . . . because . . . because. . . ."

He halted and could not speak on. But even half-paralyzed, he looked from one to another in a sort of driven frenzy.

"Because they don't want to be saved!" he blurted out all in one breath.

Again he was still, looking from side to side like one who fears he has been trapped by his own foolishness.

"Because they don't want to be saved!" he repeated, seeking assurance in speech. "That is the deliberate intent of this myth, that is its practical effect, not to be saved, not ever to go back to the land of their fathers. . . . I don't say that it is conscious, necessarily. But if it's unconscious, it's even worse. . . . They *really* believe redemption will come, I repeat it, again, they believe in all truth and sincerity, they hope for it, aspire to it, and yet they *intend* that it should not come. This is not deceit, it's not duplicity at all. I'm sure of it, I'm sure of it. . . . Here something is at work beneath the surface, something rooted in the depths of their heart, something unconscious. . . . It's not for nothing that that myth became so beloved among the people, and holds such sway that they became like some kind of poets, not concerned at all with the world as it is, but altogether given up to dream and legend. Two thousand years it has consoled them, and for two thousand more they will live by its warmth, in dream, in mourning, in expectation, and in secret fear of it, and never will they tire. And that's the whole essence of Judaism, the whole character of Israel, and of its love of Zion, and the holiness of the land, and the holy tongue, and the end of days, and everything altogether. . . . But let's leave this now. For what if they really have something to fear? What if it's true that Judaism can manage to survive somehow in Exile, but here, in the Land of Israel, it's doubtful? . . . What if this country is fated to take the place of religion, if it's a grave danger to the survival of the people, if it replaces an enduring center with a transient center, a solid foundation with a vain and empty foundation? And what if this Land of Israel is a stumbling block and a catastrophe, if it's the end and finish of everything? . . ."

A queer, weary and ill-defined smile flickered on his lips.

"Well? . . ." He turned his eyes on them as though waiting for an answer. "What if they're right? What if their instinct doesn't deceive them? . . . Just see how here, here, in Israel, they are against us, all the old settlers, all those pious old Jews, simple Jews like all those that ever lived in any other place or time. Don't their very faces tell us plainly: 'We are no Zionists, we are God-fearing Jews! We don't want a Hebrew State or a national home. What we want is to go up peacefully to be buried on the Mount of Olives, or down to pray at the Wailing Wall undisturbed. . . .' Now, that means something! I won't talk about our Mizrachi people, those little naïve semi-sophisticates of our Zionist movement. I'm speaking about the people, the people of the root and foundation. Well, then? . . . I'll tell you!

To my mind, if I am right, Zionism and Judaism are not at all the same, but two things quite different from each other, and maybe even two things directly opposite to each other! At any rate, far from the same. When a man can no longer be a Jew, he becomes a Zionist. I am not exaggerating. The Biluim were primarily very imperfect Jews. It wasn't the pogroms that moved them —that's all nonsense, the pogroms—they were falling apart inside, they were rootless and crumbling within. Zionism begins with the wreckage of Judaism, from the point where the strength of the people fails. That's a fact! Nobody has yet begun to understand Zionism. It is far deeper, far more pregnant with vast and fateful consequences than appears on the surface, or than people say. Herzl expressed no more than the rudiments of it. Ahad Ha'am said nothing at all, just another idea that came into the head of an inquiring Jew. At most, he went around advising Jews who had somehow determined to establish a new community that they'd do better to set up a Jewish study circle or build a school or cemetery first. . . . What?" He turned to one of the committee who had opened his mouth to speak.

"Oh nothing," the interrupter chuckled, "I just remembered something. I had an uncle, he was a clever fellow. The Bolsheviks killed him. For nothing, just killed him. He used to say: 'Ahad Ha'am is the Habad school of Zionism.' "

The committee enjoyed the remark, but the chairman felt it his duty to reprove him. "Don't interrupt!" he said.

Yudka may not have heard, or may not have understood; he stood bemused and smiling.

"I'll finish soon," he said with a deprecating smile.

For a while he waited, collected his thoughts and sought a new beginning.

"Yes. . . ." He coughed two or three times. "Right away. . . . What was it I wanted to say? That is . . . about Zionism. Yes! In a word, no one has yet said the right . . . the . . . the hidden, the deepest . . . no one has revealed, or explained, fully . . . just talk, elementary things, banalities, you know, empty, meaningless phrases. . . ."

"Oh, they've explained," one of the committee broke in, jesting. "The Brith Shalom, the wise men of the University and all the other little professors. . . ."

"You can't prove anything by idiots," another spoke up in an offhand manner.

"Ernest Fig . . ." went on the first, referring to a public figure who was regarded as something of a fool and an exhibitionist.

"Ernst is' nicht fähig, und Fäig is' nicht ernst . . ." rejoined the first with a witticism.

"I ask you not to interrupt and not to talk across the table!" The chairman straightened up and took over control. "Please continue."

"All right." Yudka began again, struggling with the words. "Of course I'm not the one to say what Zionism is. I'm not the man for it. Even though I've wracked my brain and thought about it for a long time. But that's not important. . . . One thing is clear. Zionism is not a continuation, it is no medicine for an ailment. That's nonsense! It is uprooting and destruction, it's the opposite of what has been, it's the end. . . . It has almost nothing to do with the people, a thoroughly non-popular movement, much more apart from the people than the Bund, more than assimilationism, more even than communism. The fact is, it turns away from the people, is opposed to it, goes against its will and spirit, undermines it, subverts it and turns off in a different direction, to a certain distant goal; Zionism, with a small group at its head, is the nucleus of a different people. . . . Please note that: not new or restored, but *different*. And if anyone doesn't agree, well, I'm very sorry, but either he's mistaken or he's deluding himself. What? Perhaps it isn't so? I believe that this land of Israel already is no longer Jewish. Even now, let alone in the future. Time will tell, as they say. That's its hidden core, that's the power it will yet unfold. Yes! At any rate, it's a different Judaism, if you choose to fool yourselves and keep that name, but certainly not the same as survived for two thousand years, not at all the same. That is . . . well, nothing. You understand? And nothing will help, neither grandfathers and grandmothers nor antiquities, nor even Hebrew literature which has grown like a crust on the past, and clings to the old small towns of our Exile. All wasted! *Kaput!* I'll take the liberty of mentioning one detail, not directly related, but it has some bearing, a tangential bearing . . . a fine expression, you know," his lips twisted in a smiling grimace. "So round and smooth: tangential. . . . Well, then, it's well known that we're all ashamed to speak Yiddish, as though it were some sort of disgrace. I intentionally said 'ashamed.' Not that we dislike, or fear, or refuse, but we're ashamed. But Hebrew, and none other than Sephardic Hebrew, strange and foreign as it is, we speak boldly, with a kind of pride or vanity, even though it isn't as easy and natural as Yiddish, and even though it hasn't the vitality, the sharp edge and healthy vigor of our folk language. What's the meaning of this? What's the reason for it? For no reason at all, just to take on such an immense burden? But it's quite simple: This community is not continuing anything, it is different, something entirely specific, almost not Jewish, practically not Jewish at all. . . . In the same way, we are ashamed to be called by the ordinary, customary

Jewish names, but we are proud to name ourselves, say, Artzieli or Avnieli. Haimovitch, you will agree, that's a Jewish name, entirely too Jewish, but Avnieli—that's something else again, the devil knows what, but it has a strange sound, not Jewish at all, and so proud! That's why we have so many Gideons, Ehuds, Yigals, Tirzahs . . . what? . . . And it doesn't matter that we had the same kind of thing before, that was with the assimilationists, that's easy to understand. There we were living among strangers, people who were different and hostile, and we had to hide, to dissimulate, to be lost to sight, to appear different from what we really were. But here? Aren't we among our own, all to ourselves, with no need for shame, or for hiding, or anyone to hide from? Well then, how do you expect to understand this? . . . That's it! That's the whole thing, point by point. It's obvious, no continuity but a break, the opposite of what was before, a new beginning. . . . A little detail, quite unimportant, it didn't deserve going into so much, but it is a symptom of far more . . . I've gone into side issues. I won't keep you much longer. I'm finishing. In a word, this is the aim: one people, and above all, a people creating its history for itself, with its own strength and by its own will, not others making it for it, and history, not the chronicles of a congregation, anything but *chronicles,* that's how it stands. For a people that doesn't live in its own land and doesn't rule itself has no history. That's my whole idea. I've already told you and I repeat again, and I'll say it again and again, day and night . . . is it clear? Is it clear?" And all at once his words ran together and his voice broke and sputtered with feeling, his eyes flickered to and fro like one who doesn't know which way to go. "With this I've said a great deal, the whole thing . . . everything I had on my mind . . . and now I don't want to say anything more. I have nothing more to add. . . . Enough!"

He noisily pulled back a chair and cast himself heavily into it, wiping the sweat off his face with his palm, and sat there all in a turmoil, with his face flaming, his heart pounding, and his temples throbbing.

It grew quiet, like the stillness after a quarrel. The men were silent and sat uncertainly with changed faces, not sure in their hearts nor easy in their minds, as though in doubt whether something might not be lost or lacking, or as if they were in mid-passage between where they had been and where they were going.

Then the chairman lifted his eyes and spoke with a certain strain: "Have you finished?"

At that, Yudka sprang to his feet with a jerk.

"Right away, right away . . ." He spoke hastily and with some panic. "I said much too much. . . . That's not how I meant it, not the way I thought. It came out by itself. The devil knows how . . . such nonsense! Trifles, side issues like that, about Yiddish there, and the names. . . . It was ridiculous, quite unnecessary. I see it myself. . . . But just those side issues, those unimportant details, you know, they come to mind immediately. . . . Well, it's all the same. What I mean, I really just wanted to explain . . . I no longer know how to tell you . . . the main thing, what I'm after. It's not just . . . yes! Well, now. Now to the main thing. I beg just a few more minutes of patience. . . ."

The boys all straightened up in their chairs and felt more at ease, as though he had saved them from a great worry—especially the chairman, who bowed his head and sat staring at his finger nails.

"Say what you want," he said, "and let's see if we can't do without the philosophy. . . ."

—*Translated by Ben Halpern*

AHARON MEGGED

The
Name

Aharon Megged was born
in Poland in 1920. His family
emigrated to Palestine in
1926. Upon graduating from
high school he became one
of the founding members of
S'dot Yam, a fishing kibbutz
on the Mediterranean. Later
he worked at a series of
odd jobs—quarrying, fishing,
farm labor—up and down
the country. Shortly after
World War II Megged spent
two years in the United States
as a cultural representative
on behalf of the Jewish
Agency for Palestine. Since
1950 he has lived in Tel Aviv,
as editor of the weekly literary supplement of the newspaper Lamerhav.

Megged has distinguished
himself both as a short story
writer and a playwright.
Most characteristically a sat-
irist, his humor is gentle,
rarely bitter. His best known
book is the novel Hedva and
I, winner of the 1954 Ussish-
kin Prize, whose heroes, two
quixotic "kibbutzniks," set
out to make good in Tel Aviv
and learn, like the country
mouse in the fable, that city
life is not all it is supposed
to be. "The Name" tends
more to pathos than to
humor, but its central theme
—the conflict and lack of
understanding between generations—conveys much of
Megged's ruefully ironic
viewpoint.

Grandfather Zisskind lived in a little house in a southern suburb of the town. About once a month, on a Saturday afternoon, his granddaughter Raya and her young husband Yehuda would go and pay him a visit.

Raya would give three cautious knocks on the door (an agreed signal between herself and her grandfather ever since her childhood, when he had lived in their house together with the whole family) and they would wait for the door to be opened. "Now he's getting up," Raya would whisper to Yehuda, her face glowing, when the sound of her grandfather's slippers was heard from within, shuffling across the room. Another moment, and the key would be turned and the door opened.

"Come in," he would say somewhat absently, still buttoning up his trousers, with the rheum of sleep in his eyes. Although it was very hot he wore a yellow winter vest with long sleeves, from which his wrists stuck out—white, thin, delicate as a girl's, as was his bare neck with its taut skin.

After Raya and Yehuda had sat down at the table, which was covered with a white cloth showing signs of the meal he had eaten alone—crumbs from the Sabbath loaf, a plate with meat leavings, a glass containing some grape pips, a number of jars and so on—he would smooth the crumpled pillows, spread a cover over the narrow bed and tidy up. It was a small room, and its obvious disorder aroused pity for the old man's helplessness in running his home. In the corner was a shelf with two sooty kerosene burners, a kettle and two or three saucepans, and next to it a basin containing plates, knives and forks. In another corner was a stand holding books with thick leather bindings, leaning and lying on each other. Some of his clothes hung over the backs of the chairs. An ancient walnut cupboard with an empty buffet stood exactly opposite the door. On the wall hung a clock which had long since stopped.

"We ought to make Grandfather a present of a clock," Raya would say to Yehuda as she surveyed the room and her glance lighted on the clock; but every time the matter slipped her memory. She loved her grandfather, with his pointed white silky beard, his tranquil face from which a kind of holy radiance emanated, his quiet, soft voice which seemed to have been made only for uttering words of sublime wisdom. She also respected him for his pride, which had led him to move out of her mother's house and live by himself, accepting the hardship and trouble and the affliction of loneliness in his old age. There had been a bitter quarrel between him and his daughter. After Raya's father had died, the house had lost its grandeur and shed the trappings of wealth. Some of the antique furniture which they had retained—along with some crystalware and jewels, the dim lustre of memories from the days of plenty in their native city—had been sold, and Rachel, Raya's mother, had been compelled to support the home by working as a dentist's nurse. Grandfather Zisskind, who had been supported by the family ever since he came to the country, wished to hand over to his daughter his small capital, which was deposited in a bank. She was not willing to accept it. She was stubborn and proud like him. Then, after a prolonged quarrel and several weeks of not speaking to each other, he took some of the things in his room and the broken clock and went to live alone. That had been about four years ago. Now Rachel would come to him once or twice a week, bringing with her a bag full of provisions, to clean the room and cook some meals for him. He was no longer interested in expenses and did not even ask about them, as though they were of no more concern to him.

"And now . . . what can I offer you?" Grandfather Zisskind would ask when he considered the room ready to receive guests. "There's no need to offer us anything, Grandfather; we didn't come for that," Raya would answer crossly.

But protests were of no avail. Her grandfather would take out a jar of fermenting preserves and put it on the table, then grapes and plums, biscuits and two glasses of strong tea, forcing them to eat. Raya would taste a little of this and that just to please the old man, while Yehuda, for whom all these visits were unavoidable torment, the very sight of the dishes arousing his disgust, would secretly indicate to her by pulling a sour face that he just couldn't touch the preserves. She would smile at him placatingly, stroking his knee. But Grandfather insisted, so he would have to taste at least a teaspoonful of the sweet and nauseating stuff.

Afterwards Grandfather would ask about all kinds of things. Raya did her best to make the conversation pleasant, in order to relieve Yehuda's boredom. Finally would come what Yehuda dreaded most of all and on account of which he had resolved more than once to refrain from these visits. Grandfather Zisskind would rise, take his chair and place it next to the wall, get up on it carefully, holding on to the back so as not to fall, open the clock and take out a cloth bag with a black cord tied round it. Then he would shut the clock, get off the chair, put it back in its place, sit down on it, undo the cord, take out of the cloth wrapping a bundle of sheets of paper, lay them in front of Yehuda and say:

"I would like you to read this."

"Grandfather," Raya would rush to Yehuda's rescue, "but he's already read it at least ten times. . . ."

But Grandfather Zisskind would pretend not to hear and would not reply, so Yehuda was compelled each time to read there and then that same essay, spread over eight, long sheets in a large, somewhat shaky handwriting, which he almost knew by heart. It was a lament for Grandfather's native town in the Ukraine which had been destroyed by the Germans, and all its Jews slaughtered. When he had finished, Grandfather would take the sheets out of his hand, fold them, sigh and say:

"And nothing of all this is left. Dust and ashes. Not even a tombstone to bear witness. Imagine, of a community of twenty thousand Jews not even one survived to tell how it happened . . . Not a trace."

Then out of the same cloth bag, which contained various letters and envelopes, he would draw a photograph of his grandson Mendele, who had been twelve years old when he was killed; the only son of his son Ossip, chief engineer in a large chemical factory. He would show it to Yehuda and say:

"He was a genius. Just imagine, when he was only eleven he had already finished his studies at the Conservatory, won a scholarship from the Government and was considered an outstanding violinist. A genius! Look at that forehead. . . ." And after he had put the photograph back he would sigh and repeat "Not a trace."

A strained silence of commiseration would descend on Raya and Yehuda, who had already heard these same things many times over and no longer felt anything when they were repeated. And as he wound the cord round the bag the old man would muse: "And Ossip was also a prodigy. As a boy he knew Hebrew well, and could recite Bialik's poems by heart. He studied by himself. He read endlessly, Gnessin, Frug, Ber-

91

shadsky . . . You didn't know Bershadsky; he was a good writer . . . He had a warm heart, Ossip had. He didn't mix in politics, he wasn't even a Zionist, but even when they promoted him there he didn't forget that he was a Jew . . . He called his son Mendele, of all names, after his dead brother, even though it was surely not easy to have a name like that among the Russians . . . Yes, he had a warm Jewish heart . . ."

He would turn to Yehuda as he spoke, since in Raya he always saw the child who used to sit on his knee listening to his stories, and for him she had never grown up, while he regarded Yehuda as an educated man who could understand someone else, especially inasmuch as Yehuda held a government job.

Raya remembered how the change had come about in her grandfather. When the war was over he was still sustained by uncertainty and hoped for some news of his son, for it was known that very many had succeeded in escaping eastwards. Wearily he would visit all those who had once lived in his town, but none of them had received any sign of life from relatives. Nevertheless he continued to hope, for Ossip's important position might have helped to save him. Then Raya came home one evening and saw him sitting on the floor with a rent in his jacket. In the house they spoke in whispers, and her mother's eyes were red with weeping. She, too, had wept at Grandfather's sorrow, at the sight of his stricken face, at the oppressive quiet in the rooms. For many weeks afterwards it was as if he had imposed silence on himself. He would sit at his table from morning to night, reading and re-reading old letters, studying family photographs by the hour as he brought them close to his shortsighted eyes, or leaning backwards on his chair, motionless, his hand touching the edge of the table and his eyes staring through the window in front of him, into the distance, as if he had turned to stone. He was no longer the same talkative, wise and humorous grandfather who interested himself in the house, asked what his granddaughter was doing, instructed her, tested her knowledge, proving boastfully like a child that he knew more than her teachers. Now he seemed to cut himself off from the world and entrench himself in his thoughts and his memories, which none of the household could penetrate. Later, a strange perversity had taken hold of him which it was hard to tolerate. He would insist that his meals be served at his table, apart, that no one should enter his room without knocking at the door, or close the shutters of his window against the sun. When any one disobeyed these prohibitions he would flare up and quarrel violently with his daughter. At times it seemed that he hated her.

When Raya's father died, Grandfather Zisskind did not show any signs of grief, and did not even console his daughter. But when the days of mourning were past it was as if he had been restored to new life, and he emerged from his silence. Yet he did not speak of his son-in-law, nor of his son Ossip, but only of his grandson Mendele. Often during the day he would mention the boy by name as if he were alive, and speak of him familiarly, although he had seen him only on photographs—as though deliberating aloud and turning the matter over, he would talk of how Mendele ought to be brought up. It was hardest of all when he started criticizing his son and his son's wife for not having foreseen the impending disaster, for not having rushed the boy away to a safe place, not having hidden him with non-Jews, not having tried to get him to the Land of Israel in good time. There was no logic in what he said; this would so infuriate Rachel that she would burst out with, "Oh, do stop! Stop it! I'll go out of my mind with your foolish nonsense!" She would rise from her seat in anger, withdraw to her room, and afterwards, when she had calmed down, would say to Raya, "Sclerosis, apparently. Loss of memory. He no longer knows what he's talking about."

One day—Raya would never forget this—she and her mother saw that Grandfather was wearing his best suit, the black one, and under it a gleaming white shirt; his shoes were polished, and he had a hat on. He had not worn these clothes for many months, and the family was dismayed to see him. They thought that he had lost his mind. "What holiday is it today?" her mother asked. "Really, don't you know?" asked her grandfather. "Today is Mendele's birthday!" Her mother burst out crying. She too began to cry and ran out of the house.

After that, Grandfather Zisskind went to live alone. His mind, apparently, had become settled, except that he would frequently forget things which had occurred a day or two before, though he clearly remembered, down to the smallest detail, things which had happened in his town and to his family more than thirty years ago. Raya would go and visit him, at first with her mother and, after her marriage, with Yehuda. What bothered them was that they were compelled to listen to his talk about Mendele his grandson, and to read that same lament for his native town which had been destroyed.

Whenever Rachel happened to come there during their visit, she would scold Grandfather rudely. "Stop bothering them with your masterpiece," she would say, and herself remove the papers from the table and put them back in their bag. "If you want them to keep on visiting you, don't talk to them about the dead. Talk about the living. They're young people and they have no mind for such things." And as they left his room together she would say, turning to Yehuda in order to placate him, "Don't be surprised at him. Grandfather's already old. Over seventy. Loss of memory."

When Raya was seven months pregnant, Grandfather Zisskind had in his absent-mindedness not yet noticed it. But Rachel could no longer refrain from letting him share her joy and hope, and told him that a great-grandchild would soon be born to him. One evening the door of Raya and Yehuda's flat opened, and Grandfather himself stood on the threshold in his holiday clothes, just as on the day of Mendele's birthday. This was the first time he had visited them at home, and Raya was so surprised that she hugged and kissed him as she had not done since she was a child. His face shone, his eyes sparkled with the same intelligent and mischievous light they had in those far-off days before the calamity. When he entered he walked briskly through the rooms, giving his opinion on the furniture and its arrangement, and joking about everything around him. He was so pleasant that Raya and Yehuda could not stop laughing all the time he was speaking. He gave no indication that he knew what was about to take place, and for the first time in many months he did not mention Mendele.

"Ah, you naughty children," he said, "is this how you treat Grandfather? Why didn't you tell me you had such a nice place?"

"How many times have I invited you here, Grandfather?" asked Raya.

"Invited me? You ought to have *brought* me here, dragged me by force!"

"I wanted to do that too, but you refused."

"Well, I thought that you lived in some dark den, and I have a den of my own. Never mind, I forgive you."

And when he took leave of them he said:

"Don't bother to come to me. Now that I know where you're to be found and what a palace you have, I'll come to you . . . if you don't throw me out, that is."

Some days later, when Rachel came to their home and they told her about Grandfather's amazing visit, she was not surprised:

"Ah, you don't know what he's been contemplating during all these days, ever since I told him that you're about to have a child . . . He has one wish—that if it's a son, it should be named . . . after his grandson."

"Mendele?" exclaimed Raya, and involuntarily burst into laughter. Yehuda smiled as one smiles at the fond fancies of the old.

"Of course, I told him to put that out of his head," said Rachel, "but you know how obstinate he is. It's some obsession and he won't think of giving it up. Not only that, but he's sure that you'll willingly agree to it, and especially you, Yehuda."

Yehuda shrugged his shoulders. "Crazy. The child would be unhappy all his life."

"But he's not capable of understanding that," said Rachel, and a note of apprehension crept into her voice.

Raya's face grew solemn. "We have already decided on the name," she said. "If it's a girl she'll be called Osnath, and if it's a boy—Ehud."

Rachel did not like either.

The matter of the name became almost the sole topic of conversation between Rachel and the young couple when she visited them, and it infused gloom into the air of expectancy which filled the house.

Rachel, midway between the generations, was of two minds about the matter. When she spoke to her father she would scold and contradict him, flinging at him all the arguments she had heard from Raya and Yehuda as though they were her own, but when she spoke to the children she sought to induce them to meet his wishes, and would bring down their anger on herself. As time went on, the question of a name, to which in the beginning she had attached little importance, became a kind of mystery, concealing something pre-ordained, fearful, and pregnant with life and death. The fate of the child itself seemed in doubt. In her inner-most heart she prayed that Raya would give birth to a daughter.

"Actually, what's so bad about the name Mendele?" she asked her daughter. "It's a Jewish name like any other."

"What are you talking about, Mother"—Raya re-belled against the thought—"a Ghetto name, ugly, hor-rible! I wouldn't even be capable of letting it cross my lips. Do you want me to hate my child?"

"Oh, you won't hate your child. At any rate, not be-cause of the name . . ."

"I should hate him. It's as if you'd told me that my child would be born with a hump! And anyway—why should I? What for?"

"You have to do it for Grandfather's sake," Rachel said quietly, although she knew that she was not speak-ing the whole truth.

"You know, Mother, that I am ready to do any-thing for Grandfather," said Raya. "I love him, but I am not ready to sacrifice my child's happiness on ac-count of some superstition of his. What sense is there in it?"

Rachel could not explain the "sense in it" rationally, but in her heart she rebelled aganst her daughter's logic which had always been hers too and now seemed very superficial, a symptom of the frivolity afflicting the younger generation. Her old father now appeared to her like an ancient tree whose deep roots suck up the mysterious essence of existence, of which neither her daughter nor she herself knew anything. Had it not been for this argument about the name, she would certainly never have got to meditating on the transmigration of souls and the eternity of life. At night she would wake up covered in cold sweat. Hazily, she recalled frightful scenes of bodies of naked children, beaten and trampled under the jackboots of soldiers, and an awful sense of guilt oppressed her spirit.

Then Rachel came with a proposal for a compromise: that the child should be named Menachem. A Hebrew name, she said; an Israeli one, by all standards. Many children bore it, and it occurred to nobody to make fun of them. Even Grandfather had agreed to it after much urging.

Raya refused to listen.

"We have chosen a name, Mother," she said, "which we both like, and we won't change it for another. Menachem is a name which reeks of old age, a name which for me is connected with sad memories and people I don't like. Menachem you could call only a boy who is short, weak and not good-looking. Let's not talk about it any more, Mother."

Rachel was silent. She almost despaired of convincing them. At last she said:

"And are you ready to take the responsibility of going against Grandfather's wishes?"

Raya's eyes opened wide, and fear was reflected in them:

"Why do you make such a fateful thing of it? You frighten me!" she said, and burst into tears. She began to fear for her offspring as one fears the evil eye.

"And perhaps there *is* something fateful in it . . ."

whispered Rachel without raising her eyes. She flinched at her own words.

"What is it?" insisted Raya, with a frightened look at her mother.

"I don't know . . ." she said. "Perhaps all the same we are bound to retain the names of the dead . . . in order to leave a remembrance of them . . ." She was not sure herself whether there was any truth in what she said or whether it was merely a stupid belief, but her father's faith was before her, stronger than her own doubts and her daughter's simple and understandable opposition.

"But I don't always want to remember all those dreadful things, Mother. It's impossible that this memory should always hang about this house and that the poor child should bear it!"

Rachel understood. She, too, heard such a cry within her as she listened to her father talking, sunk in memories of the past. As if to herself, she said in a whisper:

"I don't know . . . at times it seems to me that it's not Grandfather who's suffering from loss of memory, but ourselves. All of us."

About two weeks before the birth was due, Grandfather Zisskind appeared in Raya and Yehuda's home for the second time. His face was yellow, angry, and the light had faded from his eyes. He greeted them, but did not favor Raya with so much as a glance, as if he had pronounced a ban upon the sinner. Turning to Yehuda he said, "I wish to speak to you."

They went into the inner room. Grandfather sat down on the chair and placed the palm of his hand on the edge of the table, as was his wont, and Yehuda sat, lower than he, on the bed.

"Rachel has told me that you don't want to call the child by my grandchild's name," he said.

"Yes . . ." said Yehuda diffidently.

"Perhaps you'll explain to me why?" he asked.

"We . . ." stammered Yehuda, who found it difficult to face the piercing gaze of the old man. "The name simply doesn't appeal to us."

Grandfather was silent. Then he said, "I understand that Mendele doesn't appeal to you. Not a Hebrew name. Granted! But Menachem—what's wrong with Menachem?" It was obvious that he was controlling his feelings with difficulty.

"It's not . . ." Yehuda knew that there was no use explaining; they were two generations apart in their ideas. "It's not an Israeli name . . . it's from the *Golah**"

"*Golah,*" repeated Grandfather. He shook with rage, but somehow he maintained his self-control. Quietly he added, "We all come from the *Golah*. I, and Raya's father and mother. Your father and mother. All of us."

"Yes . . ." said Yehuda. He resented the fact that he was being dragged into an argument which was distasteful to him, particularly with this old man whose mind was already not quite clear. Only out of respect did he restrain himself from shouting: That's that, and it's done with! . . . "Yes, but we were born in this country," he said aloud; "that's different."

Grandfather Zisskind looked at him contemptuously. Before him he saw a wretched boor, an empty vessel.

"You, that is to say, think that there's something new here," he said, "that everything that was there is past and gone. Dead, without sequel. That you are starting everything anew."

"I didn't say that. I only said that we were born in this country. . . ."

"You were born here. Very nice . . ." said Grand-

_____
* Diaspora: the whole body of Jews living dispersed among the Gentiles.

100

father Zisskind with rising emotion. "So what of it? What's so remarkable about that? In what way are you superior to those who were born *there?* Are you cleverer than they? More cultured? Are you greater than they in Torah or good deeds? Is your blood redder than theirs?" Grandfather Zisskind looked as if he could wring Yehuda's neck.

"I didn't say that either. I said that *here* it's different. . . ."

Grandfather Zisskind's patience with idle words was exhausted.

"You good-for-nothing!" he burst out in his rage. "What do you know about what was there? What do you know of the *people* that were there? The communities? The cities? What do you know of the *life* they had there?"

"Yes," said Yehuda, his spirit crushed, "but we no longer have any ties with it."

"You have no ties with it?" Grandfather Zisskind bent towards him. His lips quivered in fury. "With what . . . with what *do* you have ties?"

"We have . . . with this country," said Yehuda and gave an involuntary smile.

"Fool!" Grandfather Zisskind shot at him. "Do you think that people come to a desert and make themselves a nation, eh? That you are the first of some new race? That you're not the son of your father? Not the grandson of your grandfather? Do you want to forget them? Are you ashamed of them for having had a hundred times more culture and education than you have? Why . . . why, everything here"—he included everything around him in the sweep of his arm—"is no more than a puddle of tapwater against the big sea that was there! What have you here? A mixed multitude! Seventy languages! Seventy distinct groups! Customs? A way of life? Why, every home here is a nation in itself, with its own customs and its own names! And with this you have ties, you say . . ."

Yehuda lowered his eyes and was silent.

"I'll tell you what ties are," said Grandfather Zisskind calmly. "Ties are remembrance! Do you understand? The Russian is linked to his people because he remembers his ancestors. He is called Ivan, his father was called Ivan and his grandfather was called Ivan, back to the first generation. And no Russian has said: From today onwards I shall not be called Ivan because my fathers and my fathers' fathers were called that; I am the first of a new Russian nation which has nothing at all to do with the Ivans. Do you understand?"

"But what has that got to do with it?" Yehuda protested impatiently. Grandfather Zisskind shook his head at him.

"And you—you're ashamed to give your son the name Mendele lest it remind you that there were Jews who were called by that name. You believe that his name should be wiped off the face of the earth. That not a trace of it should remain . . ."

He paused, heaved a deep sigh and said:

"O children, children, you don't know what you're doing . . . You're finishing off the work which the enemies of Israel began. They took the bodies away from the world, and you—the name and the memory . . . No continuation, no evidence, no memorial and no name. Not a trace . . ."

And with that he rose, took his stick and with long strides went towards the door and left.

The new-born child was a boy and he was named Ehud, and when he was about a month old, Raya and Yehuda took him in the carriage to Grandfather's house.

Raya gave three cautious knocks on the door, and when she heard a rustle inside she could also hear the beating of her anxious heart. Since the birth of the child Grandfather had not visited them even once. "I'm terribly excited," she whispered to Yehuda with tears in her eyes. Yehuda rocked the carriage and did not reply. He was now indifferent to what the old man might say or do.

The door opened, and on the threshold stood Grandfather Zisskind, his face weary and wrinkled. He seemed to have aged. His eyes were sticky with sleep, and for a moment it seemed as if he did not see the callers.

"Good Sabbath, Grandfather," said Raya with great feeling. It seemed to her now that she loved him more than ever.

Grandfather looked at them as if surprised, and then said absently, "Come in, come in."

"We've brought the baby with us!" said Raya, her face shining, and her glance traveled from Grandfather to the infant sleeping in the carriage.

"Come in, come in," repeated Grandfather Zisskind in a tired voice. "Sit down," he said as he removed his clothes from the chairs and turned to tidy the disordered bedclothes.

Yehuda stood the carriage by the wall and whispered to Raya, "It's stifling for him here." Raya opened the window wide.

"You haven't seen our baby yet, Grandfather!" she said with a sad smile.

"Sit down, sit down," said Grandfather, shuffling over to the shelf, from which he took the jar of preserves and the biscuit tin, putting them on the table.

"There's no need, Grandfather, really there's no need for it. We didn't come for that," said Raya.

"Only a little something. I have nothing to offer you

today. . . ." said Grandfather in a dull, broken voice. He took the kettle off the kerosene burner and poured out two glasses of tea which he placed before them. Then he too sat down, said "Drink, drink," and softly tapped his fingers on the table.

"I haven't seen Mother for several days now," he said at last.

"She's busy . . ." said Raya in a low voice, without raising her eyes to him. "She helps me a lot with the baby. . . ."

Grandfather Zisskind looked at his pale, knotted and veined hands lying helplessly on the table; then he stretched out one of them and said to Raya, "Why don't you drink? The tea will get cold."

Raya drew up to the table and sipped the tea.

"And you—what are you doing now?" he asked Yehuda.

"Working as usual," said Yehuda, and added with a laugh, "I play with the baby when there's time."

Grandfather again looked down at his hands, the long thin fingers of which shook with the palsy of old age.

"Take some of the preserves," he said to Yehuda, indicating the jar with a shaking finger. "It's very good." Yehuda dipped the spoon in the jar and put it to his mouth.

There was a deep silence. It seemed to last a very long time. Grandfather Zisskind's fingers gave little quivers on the white tablecloth. It was hot in the room, and the buzzing of a fly could be heard.

Suddenly the baby burst out crying, and Raya started from her seat and hastened to quiet him. She rocked the carriage and crooned, "Quiet, child, quiet, quiet . . ." Even after he had quieted down she went on rocking the carriage back and forth.

Grandfather Zisskind raised his head and said to Yehuda in a whisper:

"You think it was impossible to save him . . . it was possible. They had many friends. Ossip himself wrote to me about it. The manager of the factory had a high opinion of him. The whole town knew them and loved them. . . . How is it they didn't think of it . . . ?" he said, touching his forehead with the palm of his hand. "After all, they knew that the Germans were approaching . . . It was still possible to do something . . ." He stopped a moment and then added, "Imagine that a boy of eleven had already finished his studies at the Conservatory— wild beasts!" He suddenly opened eyes filled with terror. "Wild beasts! To take little children and put them into wagons and deport them . . ."

When Raya returned and sat down at the table, he stopped and became silent, and only a heavy sigh escaped from deep within him.

Again there was a prolonged silence, and as it grew heavier Raya felt the oppressive weight on her bosom increasing till it could no longer be contained. Grandfather sat at the table tapping his thin fingers, and alongside the wall the infant lay in his carriage; it was as if a chasm gaped between a world which was passing and a world that was born. It was no longer a single line to the fourth generation. The aged father did not recognize the great-grandchild whose life would be no memorial.

Grandfather Zisskind got up, took his chair and pulled it up to the clock. He climbed on to it to take out his documents.

Raya could no longer stand the oppressive atmosphere.

"Let's go," she said to Yehuda in a choked voice.

"Yes, we must go," said Yehuda, and rose from his

105

seat. "We have to go," he said loudly as he turned to the old man.

Grandfather Zisskind held the key of the clock for a moment more, then he let his hand fall, grasped the back of the chair and got down.

"You have to go. . . ." he said with a tortured grimace. He spread his arms out helplessly and accompanied them to the doorway.

When the door had closed behind them the tears flowed from Raya's eyes. She bent over the carriage and pressed her lips to the baby's chest. At that moment it seemed to her that he was in need of pity and of great love, as though he were alone, an orphan in the world.

—*Translated by Minna Givton*

YORAM KANIUK

The
Parched
Earth

Yoram Kaniuk was born in 1930 in what was then a northern suburb of Tel Aviv, beyond the river Yarkon. He served in the Haganah and the Israeli army, saw action in the War of Independence, and in 1951 left Israel for an extended stay in the United States. His first novel, published in English translation under the title The Acrophile, deals with the experiences and self-education of a young Israeli living in New York.

"The Parched Earth" is set in the Tel Aviv of Kaniuk's childhood, a time when the city was already on its way to becoming, but was still not, the sprawling metropolis it is today. The passing of old Tel Aviv as seen through the eyes of the narrator forms part of the story's powerful lament.

I sat on the parched earth. All about me burned the evening's dark autumn, my vast evening, belonging to me alone. I seized it with both my small hands, not letting it escape. I loved it.

The short street ended in a small square in which a tree stood, a black sky hanging in its crown; in the middle of the sky there was a yellow hole. The moon had no face, no eyes, no teeth, no mouth; two clouds tickled it. "It will rain tonight," I said. In the square stood the twins, peeing their names in the sand: Meshulam, Yeruham.

Aunt Shlomit stood at the window. Without knowing it, she looked pretty in the light of the lamp that shone behind her. Her head celebrated itself, casting its own halo, singing itself songs. I longed madly to pull her hair with tenderness, but I was on the parched earth and saw an insect walking between its cracks. The house behind me did not stir. Only Aunt Shlomit stirred and ended the light.

"Why aren't you 'making' homework, Yosef?" she said suddenly.

"Don't want to," I replied. I would have preferred to hold back the answer, but my tongue would not obey; it leaped up and ruined my plan. Someone like me on the parched earth has nothing but plans anyway, plans that are never realized and remain clouds melting in the wind. Then why try? Don't ask.

I was a good child, obedient and quiet. Sometimes I was stubborn, like my father to whom everything was a challenge. If someone said to him, "Alex, you can't jump off the roof," he would instantly jump to show he could. Once, after the Arab riots in '36 he went to Café Pilz, picked up a glass from the bar and asked, "How much?" The barman said "Two grush." He gave the man the money, then hurled the glass at the wall, shattering it to bits, just like that, because someone told him he wouldn't dare. At night, my father draws. No one knows. No one, that is, except anyone between here and Rehovot. He knows that they know and they know that he knows that they know, but he doesn't mind.

"Don't want to *do* my homework," I shouted to Aunt Shlomit. I was teasing her. I said *do* and she had said *make*. Her Hebrew is translated from Russian: "Yosef, open the light!" I taught Aunt Shlomit to say "hole in the sky" rather than "moon." I have scores of names for the moon and more names for other things. On our street they call her Mrs. Hole-in-the-Moon; they are so poetic. At least ten poets should come out of this neighborhood. But in the meantime, they cackle and buy and sell. Mr. Abramowitz is already looking for a match for his daughter who is in my class. She invited me to go to the woods with her. I said no, I don't go to the woods with girls. On our street they used to sing a song about Aunt Shlomit, especially in the summer when the iceman came and everyone would stand in line. At night we all die, Aunt Shlomit once said. They used to sing to her. Especially the "pariah" . . . he was the first to sing to her:

"Hole in the moon-oo-on, he—oo-le in the m-oon, hole-in-the-moon/ hole in the—moon/ hole in . . ."

"When your father comes home, I'll tell him," Aunt Shlomit said angrily. "I'm scared to death," I answered in my indifferent voice, feeling very manly and grown up. I was thirteen and would have no Bar Mitzvah. I didn't want a Bar Mitzvah. I had this "bug" in my mind, a sort of madness that gnawed at me in the night like a swarm of ants on the parched earth. My mother wept. It was Father who consoled her. "Don't want to . . .

don't have to!" my father had told me. I couldn't explain that I wished they would insist. I saw I had lost and didn't say a word. So that was that.

"Why won't you do it?" Aunt Shlomit asked.

"Do what?"

"Your homework. I suppose you're dreaming, for a change? I talk to you about homework and you start to 'what' me. Such a brat . . ."

"Because it's all silly," I said. "What do I care about one-point-four divided by zero-point-three? We won't get rid of the British through the square root of three."

"When you grow up, you'll see it's important. Look at your father. . . ."

"I drink cod liver oil because it makes me grow, but what does this have to do with my father? He makes picture frames and he doesn't care at all about how much is six squared multiplied by zero point hole-in-the-moon." I swallowed the last words so I wouldn't offend her and so I could really laugh; I laughed so much I almost burst. But the twins were gone. I thought of their names peed in the sand. The thought flashed through my mind: God has dealt the same with me because of the Bar Mitzvah I will not have.

"Look at your father! What intelligence. You can see it on his face: such intelligence . . . You're no Jew . . . I'm bringing up a regular *shegetz.*"

"I'm glad," I told her. "Want to sing with me? I want to be an electric pole, a thorn, a grey bush in the Moslem cemetery. All right?"

Then I ran out of the yard. The ground was cracked all the way to the street, where the unfinished road begins. Everyone is building. Not a single empty lot is left. All around me stands Tel Aviv, the city that my grandfather and old Izmuzik built so they wouldn't have to live in filthy Jaffa. They stood on the hills, were

photographed, drove stakes, and behold, a city, the city
of Jews. Let the gentiles deal in finance. The Jews will
sit singing songs, making bonfires, roasting gentiles. In
the meanwhile, we need a gentile to do the work forbidden to Jews on the Sabbath. What do we do? Form
a City Council which makes an agreement with the
Holy-One-blessed-be-He. For the sake of the city,
light must be installed. That's why I don't want a Bar
Mitzvah. They say, "Emergencies defer the Sabbath,"
because they made this agreement with God. If you
can make agreements with him I don't want to give
him my chastity and promise to grow up for his
sake. . . .

Oh, Tel Aviv, Tel Aviv, Mound of Spring, your hot
winds are not spring, your spring is short and fleeting.
Two jasmine can make a man crazy, so says Aunt
Shlomit, stacking plates one on the other as she does
with the days, years, moments of her life.

"What a spoiled child," she said. "If I were your
mother, I would teach you respect."

"Auntie dear," I said, "did you see what the twins
did?" She fled to her room, and her window shut. But
the cracked earth continued to the edge of the city. Tel
Aviv began at the point where the unfinished road was
washed out by the great flood when we rowed down
Bugrashov Street in boats not knowing if the end of
the world was upon us. Tel Aviv, your winters drip and
it is c-c-cold. The houses are unheated, for this is the
East and in the East it is warm: it says so in books.
What the books forget is that once all these hills were
covered with forests that blocked the wind. Now there
are no forests and the wind is an ignorant wild devil.
Not without cause do they call you the Mound of Spring.
Sad loveliness of mine, they build you so fast that the

last new house considers the next-to-last a mound to be searched for antiquities.

Our house used to be far north of the city. Walking from the house to the city was an adventure—lonely vineyards with dusty broken branches surrounded by graves. Then the boundaries were set. One section was to be called city, the other graveyard. Now the city races after us, the wasteland retreats and I shout "Ayyy," because I was born here. If I had been born in Germany, I would say "aow," in America, "ouch." Here dreams are buried—so my father, who made frames, used to tell the Germans who wanted to hang drawings on the walls of their homes. This house, beside the parched earth, beside the ants, beside the yard with the twins' tree, beside Aunt Shlomit, between a street that is no street and another street which is a boulevard without a street—what boy is growing here? I am growing and I will have a Bar Mitzvah without a Bar Mitzvah. When Dumbo reads his Portion, which could have been mine, I'll go to the Arab village of Samuil and eat sesame seeds. They won't give me presents; fine, so they won't. They won't give me the *Complete Writings of Ber Borohov* and three fountain pens. What can one write with them anyway?

The Bible is all written, so are the poems of Bialik, even Shlonsky's. What is there left to write? Letters? Where am I going? Running away? All the ways are closed: mountains are in Beirut, and in the south the Egyptian river. Where to? The North Pole? I don't know the way. At best I go to Samuil or to Jasmine Street, or to Treetop Street, or to Raven Street. Before they gave the place a name, ravens used to cackle from the top of a sycamore tree. Once the sun died on the treetop, the ravens cried and flew away.

Where else does one go? School? There too, I have nothing to write. If I write, I remember; then it is harder to forget.

Put me in the black-sooted kerosene stove. Burn my limp body with last year's papers, burned-up news that took its own life because it couldn't run as fast as time. Once newspapers discovered time; now they can't compete with it. I wish I were no longer here, on the parched earth. For Aunt Shlomit, it is better not being than being.

My marvelous city, my wonderful city, my city of empty lots. They are filling your emptiness. Rabinowitz, the pariah's father, Rabinowitz's brothers, all come and build houses. One house, then another. They bring death to the lots. The wild visions of pioneers roasting potatoes in the wilderness, and a people becoming its own Messiah, turn into the reality of balconies. Old Rabinowitz, along with young Rabinowitz, paints his balcony the color of the murder of beautiful wastelands. The wasteland cries. How sad the cry of this wasteland in the mouths of jackals at night: yuhuuuuuuu.

"Go get some bagels," Aunt Shlomit called to me. I ran to bring her bagels. Had they not taught me what "bagels" are I would place a wreath at the wasteland's grave. But I was taught language precision. "Take the bagels," I say, "it's a tradition, my friend!" In Jaffa there are markets where a great secret lies, containing itself with caution and patience, ready to erupt like the shriek of a citrus grove's well at night. From the murky depths the edge of our dreams peers up. And Aunt Shlomit wants *bagels*.

On every second lot they build a house; on every other a billboard is erected: one side is used to post notices, the other to do what the twins did near the tree. Sometimes the sides are reversed. The houses are white, glistening shrill-white, not the whiteness of the dainty moon, but more like the brazen sun. Houses shriek of whiteness like the jackals. Every apartment has its balcony, each balcony a table. I sit on the parched earth, talk to the ants and drink the yellow hole with my eyes, debating whether to kill Aunt Shlomit or simply beat her or strangle her. Nonsense, I can't even raise my hand against a fly. Except for the pariah. In could castrate him. He told the class I masturbate at night. I don't mind *what* others think of me; I mind that they do at all. There are things which are all mine, absolutely private. In the bathroom I am king.

All around are balconies, on every balcony a table, at each table sit our people in a cloud of night butterflies, eating finely chopped vegetables with yogurt. The roofs are covered with white laundry. Old Yemenite women, their faces drawn, cheeks ridged, do the wash in giant gray basins; from time to time they pour some bluing into the suds. The blue turns white. Soon roofs will be swept into flight by the multitude of sheets that hang flickering in the sun by day and the moon by night. Everything here resembles itself, imitates itself, looks in a mirror. Winter and summer, night and day; only night is somewhat darker. Day is night minus darkness. Daytime: father goes to his work, mother to hers and Aunt Shlomit gets on my nerves. "What are you digging for in your nose? Gold?"

Night gathered unto itself and away from evening, and said to me: "Yosef, there is a bed upstairs. To sleep!" I went up. My mother sighed. "How is it in the yard?" she said, "did you see Aunt Shlomit?" "Go to the window and call her," I answered, "she's sitting in the dark, insulted, thinking about things." Then I prepared my body for the altar of night. I moved with mincing steps, touching, yet not touching, doe-like, and said, "Goodnight, Mommy, goodnight, Daddy." They said, "Goodnight my child, pleasant dreams."

I always dream pleasant dreams. I fly wherever I want to, as if I were an ant with wings. I hover above and go mad in the sky, pluck stars, do multiplication without numbers, silently steal close to Saul, King of Israel, who lost his world because he spared the king of Amalek out of pity. We are a pitying people! Mommy and Daddy have other dreams. They sleep in separate rooms and all night they sigh and groan in their sleep. Sleeping with a door between them, two parted worlds and their dream is one. What a strange lot fathers and mothers are. Dumbo has silkworms that dream themselves into cocoons and return to the world of butterflies. Tiny eggs emerge from them. A million, maybe more.

If only tomorrow were Saturday. But tomorrow is not Saturday, nor is it Rosh Hashanah or even Arbor Day, or Remembrance Day. If it were I would go to Abu-Shaluf Sumale, shoot pumpkin seeds dizzily into my mouth, drink Turkish coffee, belch out groans straight from the belly where all the years I have yet to live are sleeping. Days arranged like sliced bread, for meat, for cucumbers, for apples. And old Abu-Shaluf would tell me about Juha, the Arab Charlie Chaplin. What did Juha do? He went to the *muhata*—station in Arabic. Why? Because the wife he was buying was coming from Beirut on the train. What a vision did he, Mr. Juha, see in his mind (which was as open as the mouth of a woman) of this wife and how she would look inside his bed! What did this Juha do? He tied his donkey to a stake and waited with vee-rry great patience, *il-has-la*. Suddenly, the train was coming, the one that was bringing him the woman he had bought in Beirut, and sounding its whistle: tooo! tooo! The donkey, that old donkey, what does it do? Aaay, aayaaay, its whole jaw quivers like a whore's behind. Juha is angry at him and says, "Ya-donkey, who is this woman for . . . you or me?"

Indeed, the day waxed weary with age. That is fine speech. Mother uses fine speech. She doesn't say, "in mine bed." Father uses fine speech. My speech is wild. It comes with the hot winds, the raindrops, the sun that dries everything, manes of cypress that ask the sky questions, pointing upward as if they were fingers of schoolkids playing dumb, jasmine that inhales its own perfume, carobs that smell like a dirty joke, cactus thorns with which our dainty bodies were decorated. Mother says our land is the land of milk and honey. But what do we say? Land of donkeys and asses. She speaks from her heart, we from our eyes. We were born here, without ideals; she came here on the wings of ideals. The question is, which is greater: the thing that is, or the thing that can become. They came because they had to, therefore they could. We, however, can, because we have to. Mother has a world of her own. My world is the world of the parched earth to which I am tied with an umbilical cord. But the earth is not my teacher, and does not come home in the afternoon to ask me: "Haven't you prepared your lessons?" And of course Mother can't be fooled. Dumbo can tell his mother anything, but I can talk only to the parched earth. For mother, I am a pedagogical laboratory. And why does she hang around during recess with Mr. Broshi, the teacher? The wildness of our speech is an outrage, mother says. Aunt Shlomit agrees in simple-minded Hebrew. Outrage! An exquisite word. Such words, along with names like Rio de Janeiro, can redden a long winter night under the feather quilt Aunt Shlomit gave my mother, this feather quilt being the pearl of Broshi's Hebrew. My teacher, Mr. Broshi, will say:

Flowers appear on the earth, buds are in bloom . . .
the feather quilt having settled in his eyes like a color
film. My name is Yosef. I am the pearl of the outraged
language, the outrage of the pearl of language, or . . .
But today's not Saturday, and I must get up.

I crept from beneath the covers, bare, into the chill
of the room. Outside, the parched earth and the one-
sided street, the tree—the twins must be getting up too.
If only I had a twin brother. We would divide the world
in two and drink it up, each one a half. Together. You
have to brave the chill of the room. Like a refrigerator.
Dress fast, swallow the cold that sits in your eyes like
a bird singing songs. Gideon's brother can imitate a
bird's songs. The pariah can't do anything. If it was
Lag b'Omer I would hang him in a bonfire and run
around it, me and all my twins. It is he who sings 'hole-
in-the-moon' to Aunt Shlomit. Suddenly Aunt Shlomit
matters to me. Anyone who is being mocked is my pal.

I sat down and swallowed my breakfast. Cereal, pale
coffee, a warm roll. I kissed Mother and Father good-
bye, and slammed the door. That life was left behind,
a faint wail. God had spread himself before me. I could
have ridden on his back to the end of the world. This
is the spot where I pick berry leaves to feed the silkworms. In a moment, I was at the seashore. One step
more and I could swim to America and kill Indians.
Two waves laughed at me. They were white and full of
roaring foam. They crashed against the sand and released a handful of seashells. It was autumn and the
land, which yesterday was cracked, now spewed moist
greenery in which the clearness of water was fixed.
When I stand and look at it, what do I see? A picture
of myself, one more precise than what the mirror yields.
Mother says: look at the photograph of Uncle Yasha
on the horse. It is as if he were looking at a mirror. The

117

mirror is crooked and the clock does not tell time. Everything depends on something else. The image in a mirror is untrue, it is reversed. How much better to be on the parched earth. One day I will go there. To rest.

Autumn, enchanted, marvellous, is spread upon the seashore. Two sparrows cried the birth of autumn from the Book of Legends. The water is cool. Wind blows sand. I might find something left by last summer's bathers. All the children dash to the beach as soon as the autumn winds begin to blow. Hundreds of children from all over. What a sight—a battlefield. They scurry across the sand searching for dreams; the dreams sit laughing in the holes of the ring-shaped money, the *grush*. Arab women hang *grushim* in their nose, we hang our dreams in the hole of the *grush*; Mother, in the hole of the bagel. Father says: how do they make bagels? They take holes and set them in dough. That's father, a framemaker. That is why he says these things. Think it over; they take some plain canvas with a nothing-like picture of a chicken, one that is worthless, that can't even cackle, let alone be eaten. Around this a frame of gold is constructed. Then what does one say? Look at the picture! But where is the frame?

One child found a *grush*. Someone else found a bracelet, or maybe a wind, and flew off with it. They all find or say they find. I go to the beach every morning, betraying my sweetheart, the parched earth in the yard, giving up my place in the world to come, failing to sing my Portion of the Torah, renouncing my chance to become Bar Mitzvah. What do I find? I find someone who has found something and has run off leaving his secret behind. When I was born, my godfather said, "Today is the sixth of Nissan, a marvellous month, one with the fragrance of citrus flowers and many scented bloomings; a sun bathed in the flighty beauty of silver color mixed with lemon, delicate as my mother's face when she is asleep and not dreaming . . ." I was born under the sign of spring. They called me Yosi. "When he grows up," my godfather said, "call him Yosef and when he grows wise—make it Yehosef."

Yehosef-ele Gretz-ele the children called me with malice in their eyes. If their eyes were daggers, I would have died long ago. Therefore, my only love is the parched earth and my life's dream is to be an ant— whose lot is better, having no truck with children who go to school by way of the beach to search for a *grush* and to laugh at Yehosef-ele Gretz-ele. "Just because his mother is the teacher . . . Just because . . . Just . . ." Just because I go to school and know that something horrible will happen, every day something horrible happens at mother's school.

On the way to the beach, Mrs. Birnbaum emerged from the bushes that enclose her home like an envelope and swooped down on me, clinging to me as the sun clings to some poor creature on the street. "What happened, Mrs. Birnbaum?" I said hurriedly, rushing my words. "They were here again. The lions," she said.

She began to weep her special gems, the ones the husband she doesn't have any more kisses away—salted tears, Birnbaum tears. She wiped her face with a faded apron. A car passed. She started in terror.

"Nerves," she apologized. "Nerves . . ."

"They're frayed," I said.

"Frayed, shattered. Someone opened the sky and rained troubles on my head. There were lions here tonight."

"Lions again," I said. I was the adult here. Everyone has his moment. The shoemaker, Yehoshua, when his moment comes, sews a song. The sister of Nehama Meyerowitz refuses to give her body to British soldiers on the hill in the Muslim cemetery, at the foot of a stone engraved with scythes and swords and pictures of wild horses frolicking.

"There are no lions in this country," I consoled her. "Maybe Giladi's rabbits were scratching at the wall of the rabbit house. Maybe a jackal lost his way. What time is it?"

"High time," she said and cried a mound of stone tears.

A landslide, I thought, and was reminded of the pariah, wishing he were caught in such an accident.

"No, no," Mrs. Birnbaum implored. "I'm alone, all alone. There is nothing. Only lions come at night and roar into the darkness."

"It's the parched earth," I said, "crying for rain."

"What a country," said the old woman, Mrs. Birnbaum, whose husband did not come with her, but stayed in some faraway place.

"What a country. Every year drought."

"An awesome word," I told her, "and full of glory."

"I like furniture," she said, "because of its quiet."

"And beauty." I smiled my cute smile, the one I leave outside so Aunt Shlomit won't fall on her knees in thanks to God that I-can-be-so-cute-when-I-want-to-be. But the drought is as full of glory as an eagle.

"Eagle," mumbled Mrs. Birnbaum.

"There is 'eagle' and there is yogurt. Two sides of the same coin. Beauty has but one opposite: splendor. In the middle, hope is pressed."

"Which?" she asked.

"Of a land in the midst of the East."

"This is our land," she said and repeated, "our land, the land of Israel . . ."

"Many thanks," I said. "Mine too. I was here before, because I didn't know where to go. Suddenly, the stork

120

came and told me: come out. I came out. Know what I did then?"

"No," she said.

"I let out an awful scream, from my stomach. Father fainted, almost."

"A good memory," she said.

"Yes, but there are no lions here."

"No, no. Yes, Yes . . . that is, my father was a hunter. He hunted them in the jungles of Africa and sold them to zoos. They will come to find me, to revenge . . ."

I began to run for my life. "There are no lions here," I repeated, shouting back to her.

Nor are there bears or Red Riding Hoods. There are no jungles. Only a couple of small groves that we, the children, plant. I have planted at least four of these with my own hands. Every month, besides, I collect my money and give it to the fund that plants a tree in my name on Arbor Day, the 15th of Shvat. Holiday of Trees, New Year for Foliage and Yom Kippur of the Earth. They are slaughtering the great earth with these trees. The groves are all planted. A week later goats come and eat the seedlings. Again we plant.

Mrs. Birnbaum settled into her sooty house and I whistled myself to the beach to look for those who find things there. I placed my book on my head as the Arab women do with water pitchers, took off my shoes and hung them on my Scout belt, and walked splashing through the chill water, my feet pricked by broken shells. It felt good. I began to sing aloud, trying to outdo the noise of the sea, to subject it to my own voice. But my voice was hushed, like the breath of a swallow, by the wondrous murmur of the seaside morning, the shore, Jaffa with its towers behind, the world before; Tel Aviv, sprawled to my right; to my left, waves; fish cried, cranes cray-crayed, seashells shelled themselves; I sang:

"Tel Aviv, city of endless sky,
White roofs and the shoe-shine boys' cry . . ."

"Oh, Yehosef-ele Gretz-ele . . ." I heard the call, not knowing whence it came. Maybe God was talking with me as with Moses. With Samuel. But, He didn't actually speak with Samuel, for Samuel thought he heard the voice of his master. Of all the people in the world, only with Moses did He speak directly, and with me. But no. It was not He. Two inverted bodies came up from behind, legs up, hands leading. The twins: Meshulam and Yeruham, walking on their hands.

"What's up down there?" I asked.

"Funny. Oh, how funny is this Yehosef-ele Gretz-ele," Meshulam said from the depths.

"What if, one day, you would start to walk like the rest of us, on your feet?"

"It would be the same, but you would never know. What's new, Yehosef-ele? Look there, in the harbor. See a boat?" Yeruham pointed with his foot toward the dock.

"I see."

"It's bringing holes. A boatload of holes."

"Good it didn't sink," I said. I was clever. I knew something they didn't know I knew.

"It's no joke, Yehosef-ele Gretz-ele."

"Was I laughing?"

"No," they gestured, both of them. Their mouths were full of sand.

"Speak up," I said.

"See the second boat?" I looked. "It's full of needles. The government ordered a boatload of needles. It came and the inspectors went to work. What did they find?

Needles without eyes. Beautiful needles, sharp, gleaming, perfect—but no holes. What did they do? Ordered a boatload of holes."

"Have a good walk," I said, waving good-by to them.

I continued on my way, sang again, inventing a tune. By the time I found words to fit it I was at the fishing boats. Some workmen were repairing a large vessel. They said to me, "Hey kid . . . hey kid . . ."

"What?" I said.

"Study hard. If you're late, you'll end up fixing fishing boats." For some reason this sentence made them laugh. If I hadn't passed them on the run, my book already in my hand, my shoes rocking back and forth on my Scout belt—though I wasn't ever in the Scouts —I would, probably, hear them laughing to this very day. It's lucky that I ran from there.

I passed two British policemen at the entrance to the harbor, climbed up the hill and whistled to Dumbo. He came laughing. He probably heard the joke, I thought. "What are you laughing at?" I asked and didn't wait for an answer. "We'll be late for school," I said.

"It will wait," said Dumbo, who was a giant. His stomach was large, his nose a marvellous hump, like a ram's horn held backward.

"My mother had a dream," he said.

"I suppose she heard lions in the yard," I said.

"No, if she saw a lion she would think it was a big dog. That's why she didn't see a lion. If she saw a big dog, she would die of fright. No, she dreamed that the English left the country, that only Jews were left. She cried in her sleep. 'Who will there be left to curse,' she shouted. 'Who? Weizmann? Shertok? Ben Gurion?' "

"She really dreamed lions," I told him. "It's frightening."

"Why are you so strange?" Dumbo suddenly said and stopped running.

"It bores me not to be," I said.

"Oh, that's another matter." We began to run again.

We were almost late when we got to school. Dumbo wanted to wrestle with me on the grass. Everyone wants to wrestle on the grass. The grass, apparently, likes people to wrestle on it. But we were in a hurry. So we didn't wrestle on the grass. Not in the hallway either. We barely managed to break a coat hanger or two and, at top speed, we flew to class. The bell sounded for the last time and thrust us into the room. In class I was transformed. I assumed another expression, went quietly to my place and sat down. Ninety eyes were fixed on me. I paid no attention. I took a book from my briefcase, sharpened a pencil.

"How is your mother today?" Hedva asked.

"She's not my mother. She's the teacher," I said brusquely.

"Yes. But she's your mother."

"Hedva, by the laws of *your* logic, she's my mother because she gave birth to me, because at home she feeds me, because last night I heard her groaning in her sleep. But, by other laws of logic, those that *you* are incapable of grasping, here she is the teacher, Miss Mira. The people who bring us into the world do not always remain mother and father. Sometimes something happens. The frames change. For example, in dreams I have a different mother."

"You told me you don't dream."

"I said I don't have nightmares."

"Oh."

The teacher entered. "Good morning, children," she chimed, scanning everyone with all-seeing eyes. She sat down in her place, the blackboard drawing her in clear and solid lines. Brightness on a ground of black, just like in dreams.

To me she said, "Gretz!" her voice tarrying a second though she did not look up. I answered, "Present." She noted this and continued, "Herma, Lubianiker. . . ."

We sang a song:

> The wheels of the world (since the world
> is round it has square wheels, maybe)
>
> Grind with force as they work (stick a tack
> in that seat and you'll force the works—)
>
> In song every muscle shall sway (muscles
> that sway in song need medical attention)

We were excited. We built with all our dreams and hopes; Tel Aviv harbor—we hewed large rocks, our arms struggled with their heavy weight. It was wonderful to be such heroes. The voices soared, passed out of the classroom, flitted over the bare hills to the left, congregated at sea, raced toward distant lands, circled in the skies of reverie, played football on the sandy lot where later the army camp was built.

"Mr. Broshi taught her tne song," Ehud said. "Mr. Broshi must have taught it to her."

"Stop it. Can't you see Yehosef-ele Gretz-ele is blushing," Ahuva said.

"So what if he's blushing."

"Yes, but . . . Maybe Mr. Broshi is really his father."

"He has two fathers. Mr. Broshi and his other father at home."

"Who's talking?" the teacher asked.

"Teacher, I have a question," said Hedva.

"Ask it."

"Why do Arab women veil their faces?"

One day I was walking on Herzl Street with my mother. We went into a store to buy material. My mother was bargaining with the storekeeper. I was ashamed. Buy it already, buy it already, I said to myself. Then I went out. An Arab woman passed; her eyes, above the veil, were blue, her skin was brown, her hair was like the board behind the teacher—the color of slate. She raised a hand and motioned me to follow her. We disappeared into the secret alleys of Jaffa. Meat was sold in the streets there. In the spice market I was drunk with the smell. I hung onto her dress. She smiled at me and then she ran away laughing. I cried. Not to my mother, not to my father, not to Aunt Shlomit . . . just to her, whose beautiful face I never even saw. She was gone like the wind, false as a dream. This is my first memory of childhood. Before that everything is dark and unknown.

"Now children," the teacher said, not answering Hedva's question and raising her face from her desk and shifting it from one to another of us until she settled in a smile which grew, balanced itself on the tip of her nose and slowly covered her entire face, expanding it into one beaming melon field, every fiber smiling. "Now, I would like to have a talk with you. Close your books and anyone who has written answers to arithmetic problems on his fingernails may erase them." We closed our books and gave her our attention. A gentle gladness passed through the class, made our eyes tremble. We were pigeons circling over a crumb of bread. Outside, the sky seemed bluer.

"Every boy and girl," said the teacher, "each one of you sits here seven hours a day. In the afternoon you gather in playgrounds, on the streets, go to the swamps in the north to collect tadpoles. Each of you is born of a moment of mute loneliness." There was silence in the room. It was possible to hear the parched earth singing its lone song.

"You came into the world alone. Only your mothers and fathers were there to welcome you. Every mother and every father," the teacher continued as we listened intently, "has his personality, his scent, his culture. Here, in school, seven hours a day, we live in another world, a world of togetherhood, forgetting where we have come from and where we are going, speaking 'as if' and thinking with intimacy. Our senses are not individual, but belong to the collective 'us,' the group, the National Council, the general committee. Education is not contact with the individual. For the individual, every single one of you, is swallowed in one lake. And now (she stole a glance at me; I looked down and broke the point of the pencil), I would like some of the children to get up and tell about their homes, their parents, the furnishings in their houses, a private clock that gives the room an earnest mien, a grandfather face, the deep secret of slow budding which is one human truth, so precious . . ."

She smiled suddenly, then laughed. Her laugh glided through the room like the delicate north winds of a summer night. "I am using dreadful words," she laughed. "Even the teacher has moments when she reaches into the store of aphorisms. Please get up and speak. In this way, we will know one another with greater breadth, understand more, live a few of our separate moments together."

The children were inspired. They were swept by the stream, resounded in the wind, their hair grew furrows leading inward. Dumbo got up, sharpened his nose, polished his hunched form and said:

"My father . . . my father does something as a worker in the port. I have a brother too, Nehemiah.

You all know him. He is the fastest bicycle rider. Once
we rode to Herzliah, the two of us went together. We
hiked all around. We slipped and fell. Together. Really.
the main thing is—my father, on Purim, you should see
the funny mask he has . . ."

He went on and on. The more boring it was, the
closer we felt to him. Suddenly, we were together with
his father . . . and if we were his mother, we would
have given birth to him, Dumbo, right on the table. The
class was open to every wind. And every wind brought
a fine smell, the scent of home, delight of a tune far
beyond all the seas, the murmur of the heart on a moonlit night.

Dumbo took his seat. Nehama got up, lanky as a
tree. Her hair was always falling over her eyes so that
she would say "oof" and brush it behind her ears, only
for it to fall back again. She told about her mustached
uncle, Amiel, a watchman in the Galilee; how he took
her to the Galilee where Arabs stopped to greet him,
raised their hands to their foreheads, said *ahlan we
sahlan hawaja Amiel* with great respect. He took her on
his horse to the waterfall called "the stove" and showed
her what a waterfall is. "In the stove the water burns
with cold," she said.

One by one, the children rose and offered the breath
of their homes to the class. It was as if the room melted
with Tel Aviv, as if Tel Aviv broke into the class and
snapped all the coat hooks so that the coats flew back
home. Where to? Russia, Poland, Tunis, to the orphan-
age, to find the source of the wounds, the roots. Everyone has a root, a place he comes from. Why? Because!
The wind howls upon walls which fall under the weight
of hanging blueprints. We build the land with diagrams,
loop the ridges of wadis with dreams and build houses
to cover them up. So they will not be.

I didn't know what was happening to me. At the beginning, I raised my hand. Many others raised their hands and were called before me. When it was my turn, at first no one paid any attention. Not I, not the teacher, not Amihud, nor Dumbo nor Hedva. I rose to my feet, I was trembling, wind swept me. I saw my body stretched out on the parched earth, the twins writing their names in sand, the treetop praying to clouds, to wind, to God knows what. Among the hills I was lone as a tree. Alone, like a lone undertaker, like my own undertaker. Anyone in his own mother's class, the ants said, can have no friends, can have nothing but the earth all about. Here I was, standing before the teacher, surrounded by forty-five idiots. I began to speak:

"Father makes picture frames. At night, secretly, he draws. We have a large green bookcase and lovely, lovely books. I have a phonograph at home. On Friday night, Father arranges a concert. Afterward, we sit on the balcony and drink the sea, the thundering sea. The sea is the music, the music of the balcony. The Roth-schilds play cards on the balcony across from ours, surrounded by a cloud of butterflies. Night butterflies have private stars. They fly into light and die. How they love to be burned and die! Father plays the guitar and sings in a low voice."

"Stop it, Yosef," the teacher whispered as if trying to tell me a secret. But she was too late. The children began to smile. The magic fainted and broke. A thin rustle rose from the benches. I was silent; I felt nothing. I saw a flame; in it an Arab woman, her face veiled. In my ears, guitars played the love songs of Mozart. It was so right to drink the perfume of summer evenings from the yellow fire which played across from me. Below, under our balcony, the pariah is doing exercise like an idiot: hohp-hohp-hohp, a future champion. To the left is Gilboa's house, firmly planted. Gilboa has an awful voice. Every evening he sings furiously.

"Stop," his wife shouts. "Stop it already."

"Stop," the neighbors yell.

"Go to Hell," says Gilboa.

In Gideon's house, pigeons are roasted in the yard. Next to them lives Mrs. Birnbaum, whose husband didn't come to this country with her. Every night she hears lions coming.

"Yosef, that will do," the teacher said. Her face was pale. By now the children were laughing out loud. Outside, the sky was red, the windows drew a crooked frame for the red sky. Dumbo tapped me lightly.

"And Father . . . Oh Father draws at night," I said. "In green. He's mad about green . . . and Mother laughs. He draws with green, paints green the color of Satan's eye. And she laughs."

"Yosef!! Yosef!!"

"But, Teacher, every child told his story and you didn't interrupt."

"That's right, Yosef, but you must understand . . ."

"Understand what?" I shouted. "Understand, understand . . . it's not . . ."

"Father gets up early in the morning," I continued, "earlier than the sun, the morning, the birds, Gilboa's rooster, before Gilboa's cricket, before Mrs. Birnbaum's lions, before the pariah, and goes to the sea. Every morning, he goes there, alone, only he and the water. He says he loves the sea in its nakedness. That's what he says. People come to the sea and make a bath house of it. The sea is beautiful because it is solitary, alone, vast, embraces the sky, jumps white, jumps blue, drowns the kisses of the stars. It is beautiful because it is cold as the winter sun and loves to be alone. When Father goes for a dip in the sea, he asks its permission to honor his own aloneness. And Mother . . . Mother lights candles on Friday night. We sit at the table. The candles flicker. Two trees shouting their treetops; two candles rending the darkness. Is it true that darkness puts out candles on winter nights? Just as the parched earth drinks the rain, just as the ants build and never sing 'Wheels of the World'? We sit around the table, Father, Mother, Aunt Shlomit, Uncle Bomak, singing. If I had a brother, we would sing in six voices. If I had a brother my age, I would be in another class."

"If Grandma had wheels she would be a car," said Amihud.

"Genius," I said. "What a genius."

"Yosef, stop it. I warn you . . ." My mother's face was red.

"You have no right to warn me," I said.

"She's got no right," Rina teased.

"No right," the twins said. They weren't there. They went, on their hands, to another school where the very same things are said. In Tel Aviv everyone says the same thing in different words. That's why there is so much politics but only one idea.

"On Saturday we sing: *'Uvyom uvyooom uuuvyom uvyommm ha-Shabbat . . .'* "

"Leave the room!" the teacher cried. "Out! Out!"

Her voice trembled. Her eyes, the pupils, the brows, quaked like the crown of the tree on the one-sided street. She stood up. The class stopped laughing, stared at me. A tremor passed through me. All at once, I became conscious of the moment. I leaped from my place, my eyes filled with tears. I went up to the teacher's desk, clenched my fist and pounded with all my might. Everything jumped: dust, books, calendar. The sparks in the teacher's eyes. The stupefaction of ninety other eyes.

The hills framed by the crooked windows. The grass. Everything.

"Why did you let me make a fool of myself, Mother? Why? Why?"

I ran out, tearing the door from its place. Outside stood the row of hangers. I broke three or four of them and ran back and forth: from the classroom door to the principal's room, from the principal's room to the door of the class. If only I was the lion cub Mrs. Birnbaum dreamed . . . Now I was the pariah. I hated myself. My mother came out, deep in thought, her face white as the reverse of the blackboard. She ran after me, seized my arm and began to fuss with my hand which was bleeding from the force with which I had pounded the desk.

"What did you do to your hand, child?"

"I killed it," I said.

"What did you do?" In her face there was terror. Her voice implored, broke into a thousand fragments.

I stared at her. There was a dull ache in my chest. I stopped crying. Even the blood stopped its flow. I stared at her and, suddenly, a smile streamed across my face. "Go back, fast, Mommy dear. Go back in. Otherwise, they'll run wild in there. The children will make you miserable, and they'll go at me again with their nasty tongues. Go back. Go back fast. And at recess—stay away from Mr. Broshi!" I swallowed the end of the sentence and smiled.

She looked at me, her face recovering its color, her eyes soft, two tears fixed in them like marvellous jewels. She wiped blood from her lip and returned to the class. Saying "Thank you, Yosef," she went back. As soon as the door swung behind her, I burst into tears.

I stood outside. The parched earth died in my dimmed eyes.

The stubborn "I" was thinking, son of my father, the picture-frame maker. I have a special sort of father. Even though my mother won't let me tell of him. In this framework she is my teacher, most accursed teacher. Still, I *am* allowed to tell, to drink his spirit, to mumble hello to him. For, if Mother really did become my teacher, then it would all be possible. If it is impossible, then everything is impossible. Apart from what I will find on my own road, the handful scooped out of loneliness, mine on my cracked earth, in the secrets of my precious heart. I must know that it is precious, accursed teacher.

During the main recess, when the children joked about Miss Mira and Mr. Broshi, I no longer felt hurt. I smiled a forced smile and forgave them. When school was over, I went home, hoping Aunt Shlomit would be there.

School was over, the morning was over. The sun hung in the sky without knowing why it had destroyed the dainty autumn. It was sad. I wanted to search for autumn, for the days preceding morning. I could not find them. I stood there in the center of the sad world and knew that they had gone with what the twins did near the tree, with the dead ant in the cracks dried by sunlight.

I did not go home by way of the beach. Let the beach go to Hell! Soon the waters will dry out and then everything will be salty. If I were a bird, I would drink the sand and sing an ode to the life of the days that did not return. The sun laughed at me. Aunt Shlomit put me in the pantry and turned off the light. In my eyes, all that was left cried for its mother never to come again.

—*Translated by Zeva Shapiro*

A
Roll
of
Canvas

Benjamin Tammuz was born in Russia in 1919 and came to Palestine with his family two years later. He began to do sculpture and to write at an early age, and completed, in 1950, a course in art history at the Sorbonne. He has held several exhibitions of sculpture in Israel, contributed art criticism to magazines and journals, and edited the literary page of the Tel Aviv newspaper Ha'aretz.

Tammuz' first book of stories, Holot Hazahav ("The Sands of Gold"), a series of lyrical recollections of childhood, appeared in 1951. A second volume, Gan Na'ul ("A Locked Garden"), of similar but more brooding stories of adolescence and early manhood, followed in 1957. "A Roll of Canvas" dates from this period.

When we were small and learned that Katz Street, on the other side of Tel Aviv, was named after the father of Pesach Katz who lived in our neighborhood, we were surprised that he didn't live in the street named after his father. We didn't dare ask him about it, because we were just boys, and he was already a married man. And although he wasn't much taller than we were, he was almost bald and wore spectacles and his face was always sad, and his eyes used to dart about apprehensively. Sometimes, when he went down the street, we would feel in the mood for a joke and, hiding behind a honeysuckle bush, would chant in chorus: *Mister Katz! Mister Katz!* But he wouldn't even turn his head; almost as if he had grown used to this kind of thing and knew that he was merely being badgered.

It was only many years later that we understood why he chose to live away from the street named after his father, and why any reference in his presence to the fact of being Katz's son embarrassed him. As we grew up and outgrew him, we somehow realized that he was so short because he was unable to pull himself up and throw off the burden of his father's greatness, a burden that weighed him down all his life and drove him to seek refuge in our more obscure quarter of town.

We knew that his wife worked as a clerk in one of the businesses in town. What he did, we had not the faintest idea. We would often see him going to the grocery store or standing in line for ice. He used to speak in a low voice, in a sad sort of way, as if he had just emerged from sitting *Shiva,* and in spirit was still closed up within the walls of some darkened room of mourning, the images with which he had communed in the seclusion of his thoughts still before his eyes. The sound of people's voices seemed to aggravate some psychological wound, and he had the pained expression of one who is affected by the sudden impact of daylight.

On Saturday mornings we used to see him and his wife strolling arm in arm to the seashore with short, slow steps. They would return at noon, to be swallowed up once more in their room. The part of the street where they lived was a good place for us to play on a Saturday afternoon. All the other neighbors would scold us for making too much noise and chase us away, but the Katzes' window never opened, and they never shouted at us to stop playing.

On one occasion I remained alone in the street after my playmates had been called home for the Sabbath meal. I crept up to the wall of the house and climbed far enough up the drainpipe to be able to peep through the slats of the shutter. Even before my eyes had grown accustomed to the darkness inside the room, I could hear Pesach Katz's voice rising and falling rhythmically, with surprising assurance; then I caught sight of him standing in the middle of the floor, wearing nothing but his underwear, reciting a poem from a sheet of paper in his hand. His wife lay on the couch, listening with closed eyes. In my fear of being discovered, my heart pounded so loudly that I did not catch what he was actually saying. I slid hurriedly down the drainpipe, overcome with shame and guilt. My sandals made a scraping noise, and I dashed for cover to the honeysuckle hedge on the other side of the road. From there I watched the window fearfully. The shutter opened a little way, Pesach Katz's head popped out, and he peered around with the same pained expression on his face that he usually got from the daylight.

Obviously, I would not have bothered to resurrect this distant, blurred memory of Pesach Katz had not subsequent events made him famous in our neighborhood.

It all began much later than the time to which I have just referred. The story I am about to tell opens with the outbreak of the Second World War, when my friends and I, big boys by then, were members of the underground movement that was fighting the British. Where we lived, all the young men without exception were what were called "terrorists" in those days. We used to go collecting contributions from the people in our quarter, and on one such occasion I found myself knocking at Pesach Katz's door. When he opened, I told him that I had to speak to him privately. He showed me into the room into which I had already peeped some five years previously, and invited me to sit down. It was the first time I had met him personally, and his courtesy embarrassed me; I quickly proceeded to discourse at some length on the purpose of my visit. He heard me out gravely, and as he listened his eyes grew sadder and sadder.

"It grieves me deeply," he said, "to see a Jewish boy spending his days in such activities."

"That is our duty," I replied sharply. "Everyone has to do his bit. And how can you say . . ." My voice trailed off, as he seemed to be on the verge of tears.

"No, you have not understood me," Pesach Katz whispered, and added: "Of course we all have to do something for our nation, but killing is forbidden . . . You are taking human lives, and that is not being true to the nature of our people . . . it is forbidden. We are not like the other nations. We have to conquer with the spirit, not by force . . . Our cry will be heard from out of the silent depths. A still, small voice . . ."

He fixed his eyes on me as if hoping that I might agree with him and repent then and there.

"So you don't want to give?" I asked dryly.

"Give?" he repeated as if unable to grasp what I

meant. "No, no! Of course not. I want to save you, to warn you . . . It is forbidden, we are not allowed to . . ."

I was not used to this kind of talk in our neighborhood. Most of the people used to give readily, and the few who refused would do so in no uncertain terms and kick me out of the house. I was at a loss how to bring the awkward situation to a close, and repeated with rather stupid insistence:

"So you don't want to give?"

He raised his hands in a helpless gesture, and dropped them back in his lap.

"Well then, Shalom!" I said and got up to go.

"Go in peace," murmured Pesach Katz. "Don't judge me . . . Think over what I have said. Mend your ways . . . You are a son of Israel."

I flung another "Shalom!" in his face and made my escape.

About that time the World War began. One evening, at the local kiosk, I overheard someone remark derisively that Pesach Katz had gone to enlist in the British Army and had been turned down because he was so miserably scraggy. A few days later he disappeared from our quarter. Not having seen him for some time, the grocer asked Pesach's wife what had happened to him; so we learned that he had gone to work in a British army camp somewhere in the country, and was employed as a bookkeeper in army stores.

After a while, he began to come home for Saturday leave. During the six years of the war, it was a familiar sight to see Pesach Katz emerge from the last bus on Fridays, make for his house at a sober pace, and be swallowed up in the darkness of his room until Sunday morning, when he would come out again, board the first bus, and disappear for another week. And here I come to the crux of my story.

Pesach Katz's six years in an army camp left their mark on him. His voice became less diffident, and the light of day ceased to distress him. Before the war, he used to hug the walls of the houses as he went down the road; now he walked in the middle of the street like a man. It was these changes that I noticed in him that led me to believe the story I heard from Shaya Goldberg; otherwise I would surely have said that Shaya was making it up . . . But let's go back to the beginning.

The desk at which I am writing this story was made for me by Shaya Goldberg, the carpenter. I was out of work that summer after the World War, and developed the habit of sitting in Shaya Goldberg's workshop and watching him make my table. That was when I heard about the beginning of the Pesach Katz affair.

One day, Shaya told me, Pesach Katz came to his workshop and asked him to go with him to his house. He said he had a business proposition to put to him. The carpenter, who until that day had barely exchanged two words with Pesach Katz, was more than a little surprised, but—as he was a good-natured fellow and afraid of hurting anyone's feelings (he used to contribute to the underground although he was not wholeheartedly with us, as I learned from him several years later)—he accompanied Pesach home.

"Would you be so kind, sir, as to feel this cloth and tell me what you think of it?" said Katz.

Shaya Goldberg put his hand on a large, bulky roll of cloth that lay in the middle of the room and felt it.

"First-class tent-canvas," he said. "How did you get hold of it? You don't see the likes of it on the market these days."

"Ha! You're surprised," cried Pesach Katz enthusiastically. "Prepare yourself for an amazing story, sir. Please be seated. This roll of canvas has a very strange history, almost symbolical . . ." His enthusiasm subsided into a rapid murmur: "You do not know me, sir. I do not force myself on people . . . I keep to myself, but my conscience is clear." (Shaya Goldberg stared at him in amazement.) "I have always acted according to the dictates of my conscience . . ."

"Yes, of course," the carpenter broke in, "but . . ."

"Please do not interrupt me, Mr. Goldberg," Pesach Katz entreated. "I want to tell you this, because I have a partnership proposition to put to you, and I want you to know everything . . ."

"Partnership?" Goldberg raised his eyebrows.

"Yes, yes. Partnership. But listen to me first . . . I worked in the British army for six years . . . Before that, I tried to enlist, but they rejected me because I was not strong. Well! A man can also fight without a gun in his hand, not so, Mr. Goldberg?"

"Sure! Of course!" Shaya agreed hastily.

"For six years I fought that accursed fiend, may his memory be blotted out, the arch-enemy of our people. . . . And when the hour of victory came, my fellow-workers were mostly sad at losing their jobs; I was the only one who really rejoiced, since we had beaten our common foe. Some of the men said, What do we get out of victory? The British will start oppressing us again. They won't give us any Jewish State! But I answered them and told them they were wrong, that it was not so. We have defeated the enemy, I said, and the hour of our own salvation is at hand. And they made fun of me. But there was a gentile, a British sergeant, who saw my happiness and understood how I felt . . . He always had a high regard for my wholehearted devotion . . .

And that gentile took me by the hand, led me to one of the army stores, pointed to this roll of canvas and said, 'It's yours.' "

"This?" Shaya pointed to the bundle.

"This. Precisely," Pesach confirmed delightedly. "There are meters and meters of it and it's worth its weight in gold."

"Yes. That stuff costs a lot now. I think maybe ten pounds a meter."

"That's the point, Mr. Goldberg," cried Pesach Katz, "that's it. This is by way of a reward, a tribute to an upright man—as one might say, 'the way of the righteous hath prospered.' I have been given my just deserts. All my life I have floundered in the depths, but now I shall emerge from the darkness into a great light."

"How . . . er, that is to say . . ." Shaya was still quite unable to make head or tail of it all. "What are you driving at?"

"This canvas, sir. From now on I can be a manufacturer."

"A manufacturer?" It didn't make sense to Goldberg. "I don't understand . . ."

"Why? Why don't you understand? You are a carpenter, and I am the owner of this canvas. Why not do something together as partners? We'll manufacture deck-chairs. You will take care of the woodwork and I will provide the canvas. . . . Not that I propose to stand by with folded arms . . . Heaven forbid! I shall help you with the sawing, and knocking in nails, and anything that you will tell me to do. Well, Mr. Goldberg?"

"Well, er . . . yes . . . That's to say, I understand." The carpenter didn't know what to reply. "But it's hard, I can't just decide on the spot like this, on the spur of the moment . . ."

141

"Of course!" said Pesach Katz in quick sympathy. "Who can understand your position better than I? You want to consult your wife . . . By all means, by all means."

Shaya Goldberg quickly seized upon this heaven-sent opening. Of course, he said, that was the difficulty; he would have to discuss the matter with his wife.

"And then," Shaya told me, "I had my work cut out to keep myself from bursting out laughing. And I left the poor fellow's house, thinking: 'Good that he gave me an idea. I'll go now and come back in the evening and tell him my wife is against it.' And that's what I did. I came to him in the evening and told him my wife was against it."

Katz's face fell, Shaya recalled. For a few moments he was silently engrossed in thought.

"Your wife is against it?" murmured Katz. "Why? . . . But do be seated, why should you stand? Your wife did not understand the proposal properly. At times, our wives do not know . . . Although I can't say that about my wife. Oh, no! She understood immediately. Do you know what happened that first evening when I brought the canvas home with me from camp? . . . I had a dream . . . But even before that, as soon as I brought my treasure home, my wife immediately grasped the situation and its significance. 'Pesach,' she said to me, 'we're saved.' And I said, 'I'm a lucky man to have so understanding a wife.' And afterwards, when we went to bed, we took the precaution of rolling the canvas under our bed. We were afraid . . . That you can easily understand . . . And when we had pushed the roll under the bed it made a bump in the mattress, and there I lay on top of the bump and couldn't fall asleep. Eventually I dozed off, and in my dream I saw myself on top of a high hill, looking at the sky. Then I remembered the words of the poet who said: 'The extent of the heavens at a man's head is according to the measure of the earth at his feet.' And to myself I added: '. . . and of the canvas in his house.' And right away I looked up at the sky, to see how much that was. And I saw that the sky was made of the same canvas as mine, except that it had stars in it; and when I looked closely I saw that the stars were only holes that had been made in my canvas. Then I woke up in alarm. My wife awoke too and listened to my dream, and said it was a good omen. As I was unable to fall asleep again, because of the lump that was pushing up at me from below, we lay awake practically all that night talking of our canvas, and then the idea of going into partnership with you, Mr. Goldberg, was born . . . It's a pity it's not working out . . . But you yourself, if your wife had agreed, what is your opinion?"

"I, er . . . of course . . . Yes, we might have done business, except that . . ." Shaya Goldberg concluded the sentence with a shrug of the shoulders.

"Just imagine," Shaya said to me, "the poor fool began to console *me,* and told me not to have any regrets. He asked me if I was making a living as a carpenter, and when I said that I was, thank God, he felt better and saw me off as far as the street, expressing condolences as if I had just had a bereavement. What could I say to him?!"

"What happened after that?" I asked.

"After that? I've no idea," said Shaya Goldberg. "I never spoke to him again."

In addition to changing Pesach Katz's manners, the six years of war had transformed him into a man of action. Evidently the bookkeeping was responsible for that. When he got back home, he took an exercise book and firmly ruled the pages into three columns. In the first column, headed "Name," he wrote the names of all the people he had approached with his proposition. The second column was marked "Nature of Proposition," and gave details of what he had proposed to each man. The third column, "Remarks," contained the results of the negotiations.

It soon became apparent that Pesach Katz had approached every one of the skilled workers and craftsmen in our quarter, and we were certainly not lacking in those. Within a month, the man and his roll of canvas had become the general topic of conversation.

"Has he been to you already?" the locksmith asked the upholsterer.

"Yes. And to you?"

"Sure!"

"And did you turn him down? Did you forego the millions?"

"I advised him to try Rothschild."

Even the women in the neighborhood came to hear of his roll of canvas and shook their heads: "That poor wife of his," they would say pityingly, "she slaves away in some office from morning to night, and that lunatic is giving the world an industry—a canvas industry!"

In the café where the working-men gathered for beer or coffee, they would raise their glasses and drink a toast:

"Here's to the canvas!"

"Here's to heavy industry!"

Only Shaya Goldberg, the carpenter, said nothing in public, but whenever he happened to meet me in the street he would ask, with a sigh:

"He hasn't come to you yet?"

"No, he hasn't. But one of these days I shall go to him."

"What for?"

"I don't know. I just want to."

And one bright day I went.

I honestly didn't go intending to say the things I said. I don't really know why I went. It seems to me that it was more than mere curiosity. Perhaps the memory of my transgression, when I peeped through the shutter at him half-naked in his underwear, reciting a poem to his wife, still troubled me. Or perhaps I simply wanted to have another personal chat with this Katz, son of the man after whom a street in the center of town was named. In any event, I went there with quite a different excuse. At that time, after the World War, our fighting with the British had intensified. And although our official institutions did everything in their power to please the British, all they got for their pains was the contemptuous imposition of even more oppressive laws. And since Pesach Katz had once refused to contribute to our underground funds, I thought the time had now come to expose his ideas for what they were worth. "We'll see what sort of line he'll hand me this time," I said to myself.

One day, after I had made up my mind to visit him, I caught sight of him on his way to his house. He had his back to me, and was just about to go inside.

"Mr. Katz!" I called out, remembering, as I did so, how my playmates and I used to call after him from our hiding place behind the honeysuckle on the other side of the street. This time, however, he turned around. He looked at me closely, without any sign of recognition.

"You mean me?" he asked.

"Yes, Mr. Katz. I want to talk to you, but you don't recognize me, do you?"

"I don't really remember . . ." he murmured.

"I was once at your place, some years ago. I wanted a contribution from you for the 'terrorists,' " I said with a smile.

He smiled back and put out his hand as if meeting an old acquaintance: "Why, of course! How you have changed! Quite a man." And he promptly added, with a sudden drop in the barometer: "I am glad to see you alive . . . Many of your friends lost their lives. Ah, youth, youth . . . The mistakes of the heart of the younger generation . . . Please come inside. Let's have a talk."

I found myself in that same room once more. It had not changed at all. I think that even the table cloth was the very one on which the remains of the Sabbath meal lay that day when Pesach Katz stood reciting from the paper in his hand. There was only one addition to the room: a roll of grey tent-canvas lying in the corner.

"Please sit down," said Pesach Katz.

"I wanted to resume our first conversation," I began, lowering myself into a chair. "In those days, you refused to give anything to the underground. You said that not by force, but by the spirit, et cetera . . . You were loyal to your official institutions. And now the war is over. You were very quick to enlist. You believed them. Well, what about it now? What have you to say? Who was right? Did they give you a kick in the pants, or didn't they?"

"Gracious me!" Pesach Katz screwed up his face. "What language! What sort of talk is that?"

In fact I was ashamed, but the blush that spread over my face seemed to cover up my tactlessness. He looked at me for a long time before replying.

"Yes, reality is hard, and one might say that it has proved me wrong . . ."

"So, we've convinced you at last?" I cut in quickly.

"Ah, no! Perish the thought! What is convincing about this? We do not have to take our example from the deeds of the wicked. Do we want to go in their steps?"

"What then do you want?" I broke in a second time. "To hold another demonstration in the streets? With the Chief Rabbis heading the procession?"

"Don't be angry, my friend, please!" Pesach Katz lifted his arm, as if to ward off my words.

"What then? What are you doing? What do you suggest be done?"

"What am I doing?" He passed a hand over his forehead and eyes, and when he went on his voice sounded suddenly tired and remote. "What am I doing? It is true that I am not doing anything for my nation, these days . . . only for my home . . . If that is what you meant, then you are right: my horizon has shrunk." He sighed and lapsed into silence.

"Because you didn't take the right road to start with," I said. "I showed you the way, then."

"No, my friend." He was whispering, and I had to move closer to hear him. "That's not it . . . Even now, after you have told me what you told me and reminded me of my duty . . . even now, there is something that I could do . . . Thanks to you, it is possible that I may really do . . . what has to be done."

Again he fell silent, sitting motionless in his chair, his eyes closed. I waited without saying anything. I looked around the room and my eyes came to rest on his roll of canvas. Involuntarily, I smiled. "Poor old manufacturer!" I said to myself. "What can *you* do for your people, you poor fish?"

Pesach Katz came out of his reverie. "My friend," he cried, with sudden fervor, the reason for which I failed to understand at the time. "You have given me the push that I needed . . . I have to thank you. Let me shake your hand."

He got up and I quickly followed suit, surprised and curious to hear what he was going to say. He pumped my arm up and down. "Tomorrow at the same time, I shall have news for you. Please come back tomorrow."

That evening, after I left and before his wife got back from work, he sat down at the table, took a clean sheet of paper and, casting a long, sad glance at the roll of canvas reposing in the corner of the room, he waved his hand in the air as if to dispel any doubts he might still have, and wrote:

His Excellency the High Commissioner, Jerusalem.

> *Your Excellency,*
>
> *I gave six years of my life for victory over our common enemy. I hoped and believed that with victory would come salvation for my people as well, and the gates of the country would be thrown open to our brethren in the Diaspora. And this is what we got—the White Paper, which is a betrayal of my people.*
>
> *Therefore, grieved and deeply offended, I beg to return the property I received from the British Government on the termination of my services with the army. Kindly inform me where to apply in this matter.*
>
> *Yours, bitterly disappointed,*
>
> *Pesach Katz*

He waited two weeks before a reply arrived from the High Commissioner's office. It read:

Mr. P. Katz, Tel-Aviv.

Dear Sir,

I have been requested by His Excellency to inform you that in matters concerning the return of property, application should be made to the office of the Official Receiver.

It took Pesach Katz two days to find out where the office of the Official Receiver was. With head held high and looking very determined, Pesach addressed himself to the first official he came across in the long hall, and explained his business.

The official was, of course, not an Englishman, but a Jew in British employ. When he grasped what it was all about, he glanced quickly to the right and to the left, and then signaled to Pesach Katz to keep quiet and step out into the corridor with him. When they were outside, he pulled him into a dark corner under the staircase, and whispered in his ear:

"What you are suggesting is very dangerous . . . You could be thrown into jail for just the few words you've said to me . . . But *I* understand you perfectly, just how angry you are with the British, and I'm prepared to do you a personal favor and take this material from you. But you must not tell anyone, on your word of honor."

The official spoke in a hurried whisper, wiping his nicotine-yellowed moustache as he did so, his eyes darting about on all sides.

All Pesach Katz asked was: "But you will tell the British everything I explained to you?"

"Sure, sure!" the man promised hastily. "Only you

just keep completely mum, for your own safety . . . that's the main thing."

"Very well," said Pesach Katz. "I have just one request to make to you. I haven't the strength to carry the canvas. Could you come to my house for it?"

"Of course," said the official. "You don't dare bring it here. They'd have you arrested . . . Where do you live?"

That evening, the official came, collected the parcel, and made off as fast as he could.

It was twilight outside in our street. Pesach's wife was due back from work any moment, but he wanted a breath of fresh air before he broke the news to her of what he had done. He was all worked up, he knew he had done a big thing, but he knew that in so doing he had harmed his wife. He wanted to gather courage and confidence. Had he had a son at home, a little child, maybe he would have stroked its head now, without saying anything, and drawn courage from the sensation of being a father who would not have to be ashamed when the day came and his son asked: What did you do in those days for your people and your country?

But as he had no son, he went outside and strode swiftly towards a group of children playing in the street. He wanted to stroke one of their heads in passing. His heart was full to overflowing.

—*Translated by K. Kaplan*

S. YIZHAR

The
Prisoner

S. Yizhar was born in 1916 of a pioneering Palestinian family; his father was a farmer, as was his uncle, Moshe Smilansky, a well known writer of Hebrew short stories and romances. Yizhar was raised in Rehovot, the town in which he now lives. A teacher by profession, he is an active figure in Mapai, the Israel Labor Party, and has served as a member of the Knesset, the Israeli parliament.

Yizhar's first story appeared in 1938. It has been followed by several volumes of fiction, among them the novella Shayara Shel Hatsot ("The Midnight Convoy"), winner of the 1950 Brenner Prize, and Y'may Ziklag ("The Days of Ziklag"), a long novel about the Israeli War of Independence published in 1958, whose difficult style and outspoken iconoclasm became a literary cause célèbre. "The Prisoner" was written shortly after the War. It takes place in the late summer of 1948, a period when the Jewish forces were on the offensive throughout most of the country.

151

Shepherds and their flocks were scattered on the rocky hillsides, among the woods of low terebinth and the stretches of wild rose, and even along the swirling contours of valleys foaming with light, with those golden-green sparks of rustling summer grain under which the clodded earth, smelling of ancient soil, ripe and good, crumples to grey flour at a foot's touch; on the plains and in the valleys flocks of sheep were wandering; on the hilltops, dim, human forms, one here and one there, sheltered in the shade of olive trees: it was clear that we could not advance without arousing excitement and destroying the purpose of our patrol.

We sat down on the rocks to rest a bit and to cool our dripping sweat in the sunlight. Everything hummed of summer, like a golden beehive. A whirlpool of gleaming mountain-fields, olive hills, and a sky ablaze with an intense silence blinded us for moments and so beguiled our hearts that one longed for a word of redeeming joy. And yet in the midst of the distant fields shepherds were calmly leading their flocks with the tranquil grace of fields and mountains and a kind of easy unconcern—the unconcern of good days when there was yet no evil in the world to forewarn of other evil things to come. In the distance quiet flocks were grazing, flocks from the days of Abraham, Isaac, and Jacob. A far-off village, wreathed with olive trees of dull copper, was slumbering in the curves of hills gathered like sheep against the mountains. But designs of a different sort cast their diagonal shadows across the pastoral scene!

For a long time our sergeant had been carefully peering through his fieldglasses, sucking his cigarette, and weaving plans. There was no point in going further, but to return empty-handed was out of the question. One

of the shepherds, or at least one of their boys, or maybe
several of them, had to be caught. Some action had
to be taken, or something be burned. Then we could
return with something concrete to point to, something
accomplished.

The sergeant, of medium height, had thick brows
which met over his deep-sunken eyes; his cap, pushed
back on his balding head, exposed a receding forehead
and damp, limp wisps of hair to the wind. We followed
his gaze. Whatever it was that he saw, we saw a world
of green-wool hills, a wasteland of boulders, and far-off
olive trees, a world crisscrossed with golden valleys of
grain—the kind of world that fills you with peace,
while a lust for good, fertile earth urged one to return
to back-bending work, to grey dust, to the toil of the
burning summer: not to be one of the squad which the
sergeant was planning to thrust bravely into the calm
of the afternoon.

And, in fact, he was about ready to take action because just then we noticed a shepherd and his flock
resting in the leveled grain in the shadow of a young,
green oak. Instantly a circle was described in the world:
outside the circle, everything else; inside, one man, iso-
lated, to be hunted alive. And the hunters were already
off. Most of the platoon took cover in the thickets and
rocks to the right, while the sergeant and two or three
others made an encircling movement down to the left
in order to surprise their prey and drive him into the
arms of the ambush above. Amidst the tender, golden
grain we stole like thieves, trampling the bushes which
the sheep had cropped so closely, our hobnails harshly
kissing the warm, grey, sandy soil. We "took advantage"
of the "terrain," of the "vegetation," of the protection
offered by "natural cover," and we burst into a gallop
toward the man seated on a rock in the shadow of the

oak. Panic-stricken, he jumped to his feet, threw down his staff, lurched forward senselessly like a trapped gazelle, and disappeared over the top of the ridge right into the arms of his hunters.

What a laugh! What fun! Our sergeant hadn't recovered before another bright idea struck him, astonishingly bold and shrewd: take the sheep too! A complete operation! Drunk with satisfaction, he slapped one palm against the other and then rubbed them together as if to say, "This will be the real thing!" Someone else, smacking his lips, said: "Boy, what a stew that will be, I'm telling you—." And we willingly turned to the task, roused to a genuine enthusiasm by the flush of victory and the prospect of reward. "Come on! Let's get going!"

But the noise frightened the sheep. Some tossed their heads, some tried to flee, others waited to see what the rest would do. But who knew anything about handling sheep? We were ridiculous and that's just what our sergeant said, and he claimed that "schlemiels" and idiots like us could only mess up a good thing. Raising his voice, he began calling the sheep with a br-r-r and gr-r-r and a ta-ah-ta-ah and all the other noises and signs used by shepherds and their flocks from the beginning of time. He told one of the men to get in front of the sheep and to bleat, while some of us paired off on either side, brandishing our rifles like staffs and striking up a shepherd's tune, and three or more brought up the rear the same way. Thus, with a show of energy and wild laughter, we might overcome our hesitation, and be, in fact, soldiers.

In the confusion we had forgotten that behind a rock on the slope, huddled between two rifle butts and two pairs of spiked boots, sat our prisoner shivering like a rabbit—a man of about forty, with a moustache droop-

ing at the corners of his mouth, a silly nose, slightly
gaping lips, and eyes . . . but these were bound with
his *kaffiyah* so that he couldn't see, although what he
might have seen I don't know.

"Stand up," he was told as our sergeant came over
to take a good look at his prisoner. "So you thought we
wouldn't get a thing?" crowed the men. "We did, and
how! With us there's no fooling around! Didn't have
to waste a bullet: 'Hands up'—he got the idea right
away."

"You're terrific," agreed the sergeant. "Just imagine:
the shepherd *and* his flock! What won't they say when
we get back! It's really great!" Only then did he look at
the prisoner: a little man in a faded, yellow robe,
breathing heavily behind the cloth over his eyes, his
battered sandals like the flesh of his hoof-like feet. On
his hunched shoulders sat doom.

"Lift the blindfold, but tie his hands behind him.
He'll lead the sheep for us." It was one of those crack
commands which the intoxication of battle always inspired in our sergeant, and a spark of joy passed among
us. Good. The men unwound the black cord of the
shepherd's *kaffiyah,* took his hands and bound them
with it good and tight, and then good and tight again
for safety's sake, and still again for the third time. Then
the blindfold was pushed above the nose of the frightened man: *"Nabi el'anam kudmana!"* he was ordered.
"Lead the sheep ahead of us!"

I don't know what our prisoner thought upon seeing daylight again, what he felt in his heart, whether
his blood whispered or roared, or what stirred helplessly
in him. I don't know—but he immediately began cluck-
ing and grunting to his sheep as if nothing at all had
happened, dropping from rock to rock through the
brush with accustomed ease, the bewildered animals be-

hind him. We followed after with hoarse yells, our rifles slapping our backs as we stampeded along and descended with wanton abandon to the valley.

We were so absorbed that we did not notice the silhouettes of other shepherds on the ridges of the hills, now gathering silently to peer at us from the distance as they rounded up their flocks; nor had we looked at the sun which all this busy hour had slipped lower and lower, getting more golden, until, turning the corner of a steep slope, we were struck by an intense blinding light: the smoky, enflamed disc seemed a mute admonition from space! But, of course, we had no time for all that: the flock! the prisoner! The sheep were bleating and scattering in all directions, while he seemed to shrivel up within himself, dazed and stupefied, his mind a ruin in which everything behind him was loss and all before him, despair. And as he walked he grew quieter, sadder and more confused and bewildered.

It's too long to tell in detail how we made our way through valleys and past hills in the peaceful ripeness of summer; how the frightened sheep kept tripping over their own feet; how our prisoner was enveloped by dumbness, the silence of an uprooted plant—his misery so palpable that it flapped about his head in a rhythm of terror, rising and falling with the blindfold (tied to his brow with a brute twist of disdain) so that he was pathetic but also ludicrous and repulsive; how the grain turned more golden in the splendor of the sun; how the sandy paths followed their course between hills and fields with the faithful resignation of beasts of burden.

We were nearing our base of operations.

Signs of the base, an empty Arab village, became more frequent. Interrupted echoes. An abandoned anthill. The stench of desertion, the rot of humanity, infested, louse-ridden. The poverty and stupefaction of wretched villagers. The tatters of human existence. A sudden exposure of the limits of their homes, their yards, and of all within. They were revealed in their nakedness, impoverished, shrivelled, and stinking. Sudden emptiness. Death by apoplexy. Strangeness, hostility, bereavement. An air of mourning—or was it boredom?—hovered there in the heat of the day. Whichever, it doesn't matter!

On the rim of the village, in those grey, greasy trenches, the other citizen-soldiers of our Home Guard company wandered aimlessly—their food no food, their water no water, their day no day and their night no night, saying to hell with what we'll do and to hell with what will be, to hell with everything that was once nice and comfortable, to hell with it all! We'll be dirty, we'll grow beards, we'll brag, and our clothes, wet with sweat, will stick to our unwashed bodies, infested with ulcers. We'll shoot stray dogs and let their carcasses stink, we'll sit in the clinging dust, we'll sleep in the filth, and we won't give a damn! It doesn't matter!

Nearing the trenches, we walked with heads high, proud of our loot! We fell smartly into step, almost dancing along. The bleating sheep were milling about in confusion. The prisoner, whose eyes had been covered again, dragged his sandals with clumsy uncertainty as we good-naturedly railed at him. We were happy and satisfied. What an adventure! What a job! Sweaty we were, caked with dust, but soldiers, real men! As for our sergeant, he was beside himself. Imagine our reception, the uproar and berserk laughter that broke loose like a barrel bursting its hoops!

Someone, laughing and sweating profusely, pointing at the unseeing prisoner, approached our sergeant. "Is that the prisoner? Want to finish him off? Let me!"

Our sergeant gulped some water, wiped his sweat

and, still grinning, said, "Sit down over there. It's none of your business." The circle which had formed around howled with laughter. The trenches, the troubles, the disorder, no leave, and all that—what were they compared to all this?

One man was taking pictures of the whole scene, and on his next leave he would develop them. And there was one who sneaked up behind the prisoner, waved his fist passionately in the air and then, shaking with laughter, reeled back into the crowd. And there was one who didn't know if this was proper or not, if it was the decent thing to do, and his eyes darted about seeking the support of an answer, whatever it might be. And there was one who, while talking, grabbed the water jug, raised it high over his head, and swilled the liquid with bared teeth, signaling to his audience with the forefinger of his left hand to wait until the last drop had been drained for the end of his slick story. And there was one wearing an undershirt who, astonished and curious, exposed his rotten teeth; many dentists, a skinny shrew of a wife, sleepless nights, narrow, stuffy rooms, unemployment, and working for "the party" had aggravated his eternal query of "Nu, what will be?"

And there were some who had steady jobs, some who were on their way up in the world, some who were hopeless cases to begin with, and some who rushed to the movies and all the theatres and read the week-end supplements of two newspapers. And there were some who knew long passages by heart from Horace and the Prophet Isaiah and from Chaim Nachman Bialik and even from Shakespeare; some who loved their children and their wives and their slippers and the little gardens at the sides of their houses; some who hated all forms of favoritism, insisted that each man keep his proper place in line, and raised a hue and cry at the slightest suspicion of discrimination; some whose inherent good-nature had been permanently soured by the thought of paying rent and taxes; some who were not at all what they seemed and some who were exactly what they seemed. There they all stood, in a happy circle around the blindfolded prisoner, who at that very moment extended a calloused hand (one never knows if it's dirty, only that it's the hand of a peasant) and said to them: *"Fi, cigara?"* A cigarette?

His rasping voice (as if a wall had begun to speak) at once aroused applause from those with a sense of the ridiculous. Others, outraged by such impudence, raised their fingers admonishingly.

Even if someone were moved to think about a cigarette, it all ended in a different way—in military style. Two corporals and a sergeant came over from headquarters, took the prisoner, and led him away. Unable to see, he innocently leaned on the arm which the corporal had just as innocently extended in support. He even spoke a few words to guide the prisoner's groping steps. And there was a moment when it seemed as if both of them were laboring together peacefully to overcome the things that hindered their way and helped each other as if they went together, a man and another man, close together—until they had almost reached the house, when the prisoner repeated: *"Fi, cigara?"* These few syllables immediately spoiled the whole thing. The corporal withdrew his arm that had been interlocked with the prisoner's, raised his eyebrows angrily and, almost offended, shook himself free. "Did you ever see such a thing?"

It happened so suddenly that the sightless man stumbled and tripped on the front step of the house, lost his balance and, almost falling, plunged headlong into the room. In a desperate effort to right himself, he sent a chair flying and collided with the table. There he stood, helpless, clumsy, overwhelmed by the force of his own violence and the fear of what was to come. His arms dropped to his sides and he stood stupefied, resigned to his fate.

A group of officers, their faces frozen in severe formality, had been ceremoniously seated at the table. But the prisoner's sudden entrance completely upset their quiet preparations, disturbed the atmosphere, confused the sentry at the door, confused the corporals and the sergeant; in short, everything had to be put back together again and grudgingly reorganized from the very beginning.

The officer sitting in the middle was tall and muscular, with stubby hair and a fierce face. On his left sat none other than our sergeant. One could see now that he was quite bald; the hair above his forehead was still dark but what little hair he had at the temples was turning gray. Perspiring freely, a crumpled cigarette in his mouth, he was the hero of the day and only at the beginning of his glorious adventures. Near the wall, conspicuously removed from the others, stood a pale young fellow glancing about through half-lowered lashes like someone quite convinced of a particular truth but curious to see by precisely what means it stands to be revealed.

"What is your name?" The tall officer began his interrogation abruptly but the prisoner, still stunned, paid no attention. The lips of the young fellow leaning against the wall puckered with assurance: this was just what he had expected.

"What is your name?" repeated the tall officer, drawing out the syllables.

"Who? Me?" The prisoner trembled and reached for

his blindfold with a faltering hand. Halfway there, he dropped it, as if it had been singed by flame.

"Your name?" the officer asked a third time in a tone that emphasized his patience.

"Hasan," he rasped, bowing his head, frustrated by his blindness.

"Hasan what?"

"Hasan Ahmed," he answered, now on the right course, and his head nodded affirmatively.

"How old?"

"Oh, so-so. Don't know exactly." He twitched his shoulders and slid his palms together uncertainly, wanting to be of help.

"How old?"

"Don't know, my lord," he said, moving his thick lips. For some reason he chuckled and his drooping moustache performed a little caper. "Twenty, maybe thirty," he said, eager to cooperate.

"Well, what's going on in your village?" The tall officer spoke with a restraint which, more than it emphasized his calm, betrayed the coming storm—the restraint of an original, cunning deceit, a kind of slow circular descent that is followed by a sudden swoop to the heart, a strike at the jugular.

"In the village they are working, my lord." The prisoner sketched a picture of country life, sniffing the trouble that was to come.

"Working, you say? As usual?" The interrogator was moving in like a spider when a trembling thread of the web announces the prey.

"Yes, my lord." The fly had edged away from the intricate web.

It was clear he would lie at this point. He had to lie. It was his duty to lie, and we would catch him by his tongue, the dirty dog, and we would show him. And just as we understood that with these tactics he would reveal nothing, so we knew that this time he wouldn't fool us. Not us. It's his turn to talk!

"Who is in your village?" The hawk hovered over its prey.

"Eh?" The prisoner did not follow the question and licked his lips innocently, like an animal.

"Jews? English? French?" The interrogator continued his questions like a teacher setting out to trap a slow pupil.

"No, my lord, no Jews, only Arabs," he answered earnestly, with no hint of evasion. Once again, as if the danger were over, he tugged absent-mindedly at his blindfold. The interrogator was glancing about the room: take a good look! It's beginning. Just see how an expert does it!

"Are you married?" He was started on a new, oblique attack. "Any children? Where is your father? How many brothers? Where does your village get its drinking water?" He wove his delicate web painstakingly, and the prisoner struggled to satisfy him; he fumbled uselessly with his hands and made superfluous, meaningless gestures, bobbing his head and rolling his tongue, getting involved in petty details which threw him into confusion and annoyed his interrogators: some story about two daughters and a son, and how the son, neglected by his sisters, went out of the house and, as a result, fell sick and passed from the world. As he mumbled along, the prisoner innocently scratched his back ribs up and down, first with his thumb and then with a knot of four fingers, stammering as he tried to find the right words—he was unbearable.

There was a pause. The sentry shifted his weight from one foot to the other. From the expression on the face of the young fellow leaning against the wall and from the way our balding sergeant got up from the table, it was suddenly clear—not that the prisoner had nothing more to say, but that nothing would help but a beating.

"Listen here, Hasan," said the interrogator, "are there any Egyptians in your village?" (Now he'll talk! Now it's going to begin. Now he's sure to lie.)

"There are," answered the prisoner, so simply it was disappointing.

"There are," echoed the interrogator resentfully, like a man who has been paid in advance by his debtor. He lit a cigarette, deep in thought, contemplating his next move.

Our sergeant paced back and forth across the room, rearranged his chair, tucked in his shirt-tails, and with evident dissatisfaction turned his back to us and stared out the window. The young fellow by the wall, looking very wise, was passing his hand downward over his face, pinching his nose at the end of each stroke. You have to know how to handle these situations!

"How many are there?"

"Oh, so-so. Not many." (Now he'll start lying. This is it. Time for a beating.)

"How many?"

"Ten, maybe fifteen, about that."

"Listen, you Hasan, you'd better tell the truth."

"It's the truth, my lord, all the truth."

"And don't lie."

"Yes, yes, my lord." His hands, outstretched in surprise, dropped to his sides.

"Don't think you can fool around with us," the tall interrogator burst out. He felt it was the right moment to say this. "How many soldiers are there?"

"Fifteen."

"That's a lie."

The bald sergeant turned to us from the window. His eyes were smiling. He was enjoying that last sweet moment of anticipating all the joy still to come. To prolong it, he lit the cigarette held in the corner of his tightly-pressed lips. The other five men in the room regarded one another with the same wide-eyed pleasure. The sentry at the door shifted his weight again.

"I swear, my lord, fifteen."

"No more?"

"The truth, no more."

"How do you know there are no more?" The interrogator intended to make clear that he was nobody's fool.

"No more."

"And if there are more?" (How can one answer such a question?)

"No more!"

Suddenly a clumsy kick from too short a distance landed on the man at an awkward angle. The unsuspecting prisoner staggered and collapsed upon the table with a loud exclamation, more of surprise than of pain. The whole scene suggested some kind of unfairly-matched game rather than a cross-examination, something unexpected, unnatural.

"Now talk and see that you tell the truth!"

"My lord, I swear by my own eyes, I swear by Allah, fifteen."

The young man by the wall was afraid that so gross a lie might be believed. He held a long stick which he drew through his fingers with the grace of a knight drawing his sword. Then silently, significantly, he placed it on the table.

The barrage of questions continued without a break. The kicks landed like lightning, more naturally and freely, cool, deliberate, increasingly skillful. If at times they seemed unavailing, they nonetheless continued.

Because if you want the truth, beat him! If he lies, beat him! If he tells the truth (don't you believe it!) beat him so he won't lie later on! Beat him in case there is more to come. Beat him because you've got him at your feet! Just as a tree when shaken lets fall its ripest fruit, so a prisoner if you strike him yields his choicest truths. That's clear. And if someone doesn't agree, let him not argue. He's a defeatist, and you can't make wars with that kind. Have no mercy. Beat him! They have no mercy on you. Besides, a *goy* is used to blows.

Now they came to the question of machine guns in the village. A crucial point, this. Here you have to lay it on or you won't get anywhere. And if you don't, Jewish blood will be spilt, our own boys' blood, so this point must be completely clear. They questioned him again and again until it became nauseating, and they gained nothing but the certainty that he was lying. Then he was ordered to describe the village's fortifications. And there he got completely confused. He had difficulty with the description, the abstraction, the geometry, the mathematics. He tried to convince his questioners with gestures, freeing his arms from his sleeves and waving them about while he shuffled back and forth. But the cloth over his eyes reduced everything to a blur of confusion. It was clear to everyone in the room that all his talk was nothing but a tissue of lies.

"You're a liar," exclaimed the discouraged interrogator. "I can see in your eyes that you're lying," and he raised a menacing fist in front of the prisoner's blindfold.

This got nowhere. It had become boring. Everyone was fed up. The cross-examination blundered along, without enthusiasm, and the kicks fell listlessly. There was sudden surprise when the stick came whistling down on the prisoner's back, a disinterested, routine blow from an obedient hand.

O.K. And now about the guns. The prisoner kept insisting that their barrels were no longer than the distance from his shoulder to his palm. He struck his left palm like a hatchet against his right shoulder and then against his wrist: from here to there. He beat himself incessantly, unstintingly, to remove any trace of doubt. Even then he was uncertain whether he had done enough or must continue, and around his mouth was the expression of a blind man who has lost his way.

The questions petered out. At the door the sentry, shifting his weight from one foot to the other, was looking up at the sky, possibly searching in the glimmering light for something that was not in the dirty, gloomy room. He feared that something terrible was about to take place. It was inevitable! Take the stinking beggar, they would tell him, and get rid of him!

"Well, that's that," said the interrogator, slumping back in his chair, eager to relax now that it was over. He stubbed his cigarette impatiently on the floor.

"I'd better finish him off," volunteered the sergeant, flicking his cigarette through the doorway with a quick snap of his forefinger.

"He's a complete moron," concluded one of the corporals.

"He's only pretending to be," said the other.

"He needs someone who can handle him," said the young man by the wall, curling his lips in a sneer at this offense to truth.

The prisoner, sensing a respite, licked his thick lips, stuck out a thick hand, and said: "Fi, cigara?" Of course nobody paid attention to the stupid fool. After waiting some time, the idiot dropped his hand and re-

mained rooted to the spot, sighing softly to himself:
Oh, Lord God.

Well, what now: to the village quarry or perhaps a
little more torture to open his mouth? Was there any
other way to get rid of him? Or . . . perhaps one could
give him a cigarette and send him home. Get out and
let's not see you again!

In the end someone telephoned somewhere and spoke
to the captain himself, and it was decided to move the
prisoner to another camp (at least three of the men in
the room wrinkled their noses in disgust at this unfit
procedure, so civilian, so equivocal), a place which
specialized in interrogating prisoners and meted out to
each just what he deserved. The sentry—who had been
uneasy throughout the cross-examination without knowing what to do—went to get the dusty jeep and the
driver on duty. The young man who came was grip-
ing, angry that he had been called out of turn. Not that
he objected to leaving: it would be nice to get back to
civilization for a while and to see some human faces,
but it was the principle, the principle of the thing! Another soldier, charged with an order whose execution
had been delayed for lack of transport, took his place
alongside the driver. Now he was assigned another
duty: accompany the prisoner! (Thus shall they go
through the streets of the town: the machine gun in
front and the prisoner behind!) He sat and loaded his
machine gun. With two jobs, the trip—God forbid!—
couldn't be counted as leave!

The prisoner was pushed and shoved like a bundle
into the jeep where the only place left for him was the
floor. There he was dropped, kneeling like an animal.
In front of him were the two soldiers and behind, the
sentry whose pocket held the official order, travel au-
thorization, and other essential papers. The afternoon,

begun long ago among mountains, oaks, and sheep, was now drawing to a close. Who could foresee how it would end?

The jeep left the moldering village behind, passed the dry river-beds, and spurted ahead at great speed through the fields, bouncing on all fours. Distant details of the landscape kept shifting to close view. It was good to sit and watch the fields now bathed in a rosy light trailing small, golden clouds, a light that seemed to envelop everything—all those things which are so important to you and me but mattered not at all to the driver and his comrade in the front seat. They smoked and whistled and sang "On Desert Sands a Brave Man Fell" and "Beautiful Green Eyes" in turn. It was difficult to know what the man who lay on the floor of the jeep was feeling because he was blind, stunned, and silent.

A cloud of dust, billowing up behind the jeep like a train of smoke, caught the rosy light in its outlines. The uneven gullies and shallow furrows of the fields made the husky jeep dance. The fields stretched to infinity, abandoned to the twilight, to something distant and dreamlike.

Suddenly, a strange thought pierces one's mind: *The woman is lost beyond a doubt.* And before there's time to wonder where the thought came from, one understands, with the shock of lightning, that here, right here, a verdict is being rapped out which is called by so many different names, among them: fate.

Quick, escape this rotten mess! Join the harmonizing of the other two up front or journey toward a far distance with the deepening twilight. But the circle of that unexpected thought grows larger and larger: This man here at your feet, his life, his well-being, his home, three souls, the whole fabric of life, have somehow found their way into the hollow of your hand, as though you were a little god sitting in the jeep. The abducted man, the stolen sheep, those souls in the mountain village—single, living strands that can be joined or separated or tangled together inextricably—suddenly, you are the master of their fate. You have only to will it, to stop the jeep and let him go, and the verdict will be changed. But wait . . . wait . . .

An inner force stirs in the young man on the back seat of the jeep and cries out: Wait! Free the prisoner!

We'll stop the jeep right here in the gully. We'll let him out, free his eyes, face him towards the hills, point straight ahead, and we'll say: Go home, man, it's straight that way. Watch out for that ridge! There are Jews there. See that they don't get you again. Now he takes to his heels and runs home. He returns home. It's that easy. Just think: the dreadful, oppressive waiting; the fate of a woman (an Arab woman!) and her children; the will-he-or-won't-he-come-back?; that what-will-become-of-me-now?—all would end well, one could breathe freely again, and the verdict would be a return to life. Come, young man, let's go and free him.

Why not? Who's preventing you? It's simple, decent, human. Stop the driver. This time no more lofty phrases about humanity; this time it's in your hands. This time it's not someone else's wickedness. This time it's an affair between you and your conscience. Let him go and you'll save him. This time the choice (that terrible and important choice of which we always spoke with awe) is in your two hands. This time you can't escape behind "I'm a soldier" or "It's an order" or "If they catch me, what will they do?" or even behind "What will my comrades say?" You are naked now, facing your duty, and it is only yours.

So stop, driver! Send the man away! No need for

reasons. It is his right and your duty. If there is a reason for this war, it must show itself now. Man, man, be a man and send him home. Spit on all this conventional cruelty. Send him away! Turn your back on those screaming slogans that paved the way for such an outrage as this! Free him! Hallelujah! let the shepherd return to his wife and his home!

There is no other way. Years might pass before he is set free, by some magic, to return to the hills to look for his wife and family; meanwhile, they have become fugitives fleeing misery and disease—mere human dust. Who knows what can happen in this meanwhile, and where? Perhaps, in this meanwhile someone will decide to get rid of him, to finish him off for some reason or even for no reason at all.

Why don't you make the driver stop? It's your duty, a duty from which there is no escape. It's so clear that it's hard to wait for you to act. Here you must rise and act. Say a word to the driver. Tell him and his companion that this was the order. Tell them a story, tell them something—or don't even bother. Just let it happen. You are going to face the sentence, that's sure. Let him go!

(How can I? He's not mine. He's not in my hands. It's not true that I'm his master. I'm only a messenger and nothing more. Is it my fault? Am I responsible for the hard hearts of others?)

That's enough. That's a shameful escape. That's the way every son-of-a-bitch escapes from a fateful decision and hides himself behind "I have no choice," those filthy and shopworn words. Where is your honor? Where is this independence of thought you boast about? Where is freedom, hurrah for freedom, the love of freedom! Free him! And what's more, prepare to be sentenced for this "crime." It's an honor. Where are they now, all your words, your protests, your rebellions about pettiness, about oppression, about the ways to truth and freedom? Today is your day of payment. And you shall pay, my son. It's in your hands.

(I can't. I'm nothing but a messenger. What's more, there's a war, and this man is from the other side. Perhaps he is a victim of the intrigues of his people but, after all, I am forbidden and have not the power to free him. What would happen if we all started to set prisoners free? Who knows, maybe he really knows something important and only puts on that silly face.)

Is that what you really think? Is he a soldier? Did you catch him with a sword in his hands? Where did you find him? He's not a fighter; he's a miserable, stinking civilian. This capture is a lie—don't blind your eyes to that. It's a crime. You've questioned him, haven't you? Now set him free. Nobody can get anything more out of him. And are you willing to suppress the truth for one more detail? The truth is to free him—now!

(It's so difficult to decide. I don't dare. It's involved with so much that's unpleasant: talk to the driver, persuade his companion, face all the questions, get into a rotten mess, and all because of a good-for-nothing wretch named Hasan, and what's more, I'm not sure it's good to free him before he's been thoroughly questioned.)

Vanity! Someone with only a fraction of your feelings about truth and freedom would stop right here and send the man home and continue on his way, quickly forgetting the whole thing: short and simple, a man of action. And he wouldn't thank himself for being good! But you, with all your knowledge, arguments, proofs, and dreams, it's clear that you won't do it. You're a noble fellow, you'll meditate, enthuse, regret, reconsider, you'll be submerged in a sea of thoughts:

171

oh, why didn't I do it? And you'll cast the bitterness of your unfulfilled existence over the whole world: the world is ugly, the world is brutal. So make up your mind, and do it this time. Stand up to the test. Do it!

(I feel sorry for him. It's a shame they picked me for the job. I would do it if I weren't afraid . . . I don't know of what. If only I were alone with him here. It's bothering me like a desire almost within reach, and I can't begin. When I think that I'll have to explain, get all involved, go to people and argue and prove and start justifying myself, I simply can't. What can I do?)

Listen, man! Can you actually think of weighing these pitiful trifles against another's life? How would you look at this thing if you were the one crouched on the floor of the jeep, if it were your wife waiting at home, and all was destroyed, scattered to the winds like the chaff of the wheat?

The prisoner has already said all he can say, told all he can tell. What more do you want? And even if he has lied a hundred times, who is he and what is he? He is only a miserable nothing, a subdued, shrivelled creature, a mask wrapped in a cloth, someone shrunken and stooped like a worthless sack, frightened, dissolving into nothingness, for whom being kicked is second nature (kick him—he's an Arab; it means nothing to him). As for you, his little god, it's your duty to free him, even if he himself laughs at you, even if he (or someone else) sees it as a sign of weakness on your part, even if your friends make fun of you, if they try to restrain you, even if they bring you up for court-martial, for twenty court-martials! It's your duty to break free of this habitual swinishness. Let there be one person who is ready—even at the price of suffering—to get out of this heap of filth which was piling up in the days when we were good citizens and which is now the celebrated, the accepted, the official way of the world, embraced by those bearing the proud title "soldier." And all that was frowned upon is now freely allowed!

Oh, Hasan Ahmed, you with a wife named Halima or Fatima, you with two daughters, you whose sheep have been stolen and who has been brought God knows where one clear afternoon, who are you and what is your life, you who can cleanse from our hearts all this filth—may it rot forever in darkness!

Of course you won't free him. That's clear. Beautiful words! It's even not cowardliness—it's worse than that: you are a partner to the crime. You. Hiding behind a stinking what-can-I-do-it's-an-order. This time you have the choice, and it's at your disposal. It's a big day. It's a day of rebellion. It's the day when, at last, you have the choice in your hands. And you hold the power to decide. And you can return life to a man from whom it has been taken. Think it over. You can behave according to the dictates of your heart, of your love, of your own standard of truth, and—most important of all—of the freedom of man.

Free him! Be a man! Free him!

It's clear that nothing will happen. It was certain that you would evade it, that you would turn away your eyes. It's clear that all is lost. Too bad for you, prisoner, he does not have the strength to act.

And maybe, even yet . . . you, you right here, it will only take a minute: Driver, stop! Hey, Hasan, get out and go home! Do it! Speak! Stop them! Talk! Right now! This is the moment! You can become at last, you sufferer of many, long, empty days, you can become a man, the kind of man you've always wanted to be . . .

The glimmering plain was a thin, bright foil; thousands of acres shone like a magic loaf. There were no river beds, no hills, no ascents or descents, no trees, no villages. Everything was spread out to form a single, golden matrix, round and gleaming, strewn with moving pinpoints of light, a vast expanse stretching to infinity. And yet behind us (but no one is gazing there) in the misty evening coming over the mountains, there, maybe, there is a different feeling, a gnawing sadness, the sadness of "who-knows?," of shameful impotence, the "who-knows?" that is in the heart of a waiting woman, the "who-knows?" of fate, a single, very personal "who-knows?," and still another "who-knows?" belonging to us all, which will remain here among us, unanswered, long after the sun has set.

—Translated by V. C. Rycus

MOSHE SHAMIR

Next
of
Kin

Moshe Shamir was born in 1921 in the old Palestinian town of Safed. He was raised and educated in Tel Aviv, and was for six years a member of Mishmar Ha'emek, a kibbutz in the Valley of Jezrael. He edited the clandestine underground paper of the Haganah, Bamahaneh, *and, after the establishment of the State of Israel, the weekly newspaper of the Israel Defence Forces. Active in politics, he has been a member of the central board of* Mapam, *the left-wing labor party.*

Shamir is the author of two highly successful historical novels, A King of Flesh and Blood, *which is set in the period of the Second Jewish Commonwealth, and* Kivsat Harash ("The Poor Man's Lamb"), *a fictional re-telling of the Biblical story of Uriah the Hittite. A prolific writer, he has published several collections of short stories, as well as many plays, a number of which have been performed by the Israeli national theater,* Habimah. "Next of Kin" *is a recent story.*

The rain reached Beersheba six hours after we did. I watched the first drops splatter on the sidewalk and reflect the light from the lamppost outside. Soon the water lay glistening in large puddles. I sat by myself in the officers' cafeteria at five in the morning, drinking a cup of black tea which was too strong and too sweet. The cafeteria had stayed open for the members of the staff, who worked through the night. They were all anxious to close the case, and agreed that preparations should be made for both funerals to be held sometime during the day.

There was a continual bustle of activity throughout the brightly lit building. My own presence was unnecessary, so much so, in fact, that I was the only one to notice it. I bothered no one. Three or four times I declined the offer of a bed, though it was made by one of the friendliest sergeants I had ever met, and apparently came on orders from above. Someone had remembered to look after the guest. By five o'clock streaks of rain were visible beyond the perimeter of the street lamp, silently etched against the soft, gray morning. I made up my mind to go home. Half-an-hour later there were signs of life in the parking lot. A car drove up, men left the building. I went to the door. Joe sprang toward me through the puddles. "Come on," he said. An army poncho was slung across his shoulders to keep off the rain, and rolled up under his arm was another for me.

We set out in a convoy on the Hebron road, Joe, a reporter and myself in the first car. At kilometer 48, on the border, we were to pick up two bodies, a boy and a girl, in exchange for a live Arab infiltrator, who was somewhere in the back of the convoy. Officially, the bodies were also listed as infiltrators. The long wait had, after all, not been in vain and I began to feel better.

The windshield wipers fought the rain with a steady,

patient squeak. When the motor was cut they screeched even louder. "Here we are," said Joe, and everything came to a halt but the rain. We were on a deserted stretch of road. Joe's marker had been a signpost, planted off to the right of the highway some twenty feet from where we were parked. It was most probably the border warning. While Joe lit a cigarette, I wiped the fog from the rear window. The van behind us was a small new carry-all with a sturdy canvas roof. In the cabin I could make out the driver, chubby and fuzzy-cheeked like a boy, and beside him, an open morning paper, spread across the face of whoever was reading it.

Through the glass pane I saw the stocky figure of a girl in khaki slacks and a khaki sweater emerge from the back of the van. The first to venture into the rain, she looked down the road and began walking forward to get a better view. Passing alongside us—wet hair stretched shapelessly downward, mouth on the small side, chest too hefty—the girl strode on toward the pockmarked sign. She stopped to read it. The years had blurred its letters, bullets and stones had chipped away at them, but one could still make out: "Halt. Border Ahead."

"That's the sister," Joe said, as the girl crossed in front of him, "Tamar."

I watched her walk across the road, hands in her pockets, shoulders bunched, oblivious to everything. Around her neck she had knotted the sleeves of a blue cardigan which barely covered her shoulders. "His sister or hers?" asked the reporter.

"Hers," answered Joe. "Tshernobilsky from Migdal. His name was Chafetz. When it comes to identifying bodies," he continued, turning to me because he disliked journalists, "we prefer to bring the younger relatives. Brothers and sisters are best. Parents get so flustered you can't get a word out of them."

The reporter persisted: "Who's coming to identify the boy?"

"He was an only son," said Joe, still talking to me. "We've brought along his father, old Chafetz. If you're interested in queer characters . . ."

"The point is," said the reporter, leaning forward toward Joe, "if you have no idea who the bodies are, why did you insist on these people coming to identify them?"

"Five days ago," answered Joe reluctantly, speaking with exaggerated patience, "a family from Migdal came to the police in Tiberias and reported a daughter of theirs missing in the company of a boy from Jerusalem. The names and information were checked and forwarded. Actually, it didn't cause much of a stir at the time. The affair was considered to have—how do you fellows say it?—a 'romantic' background. The day before yesterday the U.N. contacted us. An Israeli boy and girl were found murdered on the road to Hebron, robbed, practically stripped of their clothing, without identification. We put two and two together. As far as I can see, ninety-nine chances out of hundred it's a sure thing."

"What do you think happened to them?" the reporter insisted.

"I have to get in touch with Jerusalem," Joe snapped, and left. I opened my door and stepped out after him.

The four cars stood in a row. Behind us was the army van, and behind the van, a police wagon which had a wireless connection with Beersheba. Behind that came a staff command car. I crossed the road as far as the ditch and looked back at the cars huddled together in the rain, at the dead shrubs from the season

178

before strewn by the roadside, and at the girl's heavy even footprints. Her name was Tamar, Tamar Tshernobitz, or something longer. Had a giant door been blocking her way, it might have explained her nervous pacing back and forth. But there was only the road, running on monotonously past the sign, then dipping suddenly out of sight and reappearing on the crest of a ridge, one of the foothills in the steady ascent of the Hebron range. The wet earth cast a yellow sheen back at the sky, streaking the countryside. Further off, the land grew gray and indistinct, retaining its pleasant softness beneath the falling rain. The girl had finally stopped with her back to us, and stood gazing at the distant hills, rising dreamlike from the mist on the horizon.

Joe returned from the radio car. "The U.N. just notified us that they won't be here before eight," he said. The girl turned about wearily and came toward us. "They won't be here before eight," he called to her. She shrugged her shoulders and kept on walking, passing us by and going on down the line.

Joe did not bother to follow her movements. "You're fond of queer characters," he repeated. "Here's a real strange one for you. A schoolteacher, would you believe it? Teaches nature and geography and what-not. I couldn't get much more than that out of her. We really didn't talk as much as we should have. The old man, as I told you, is all confused. Look, let's go to Beersheba. There's no sense in wasting a whole hour here."

He didn't seem to care when I turned down the offer and said I would remain. "I'll send along some food and something to drink," he said, shutting the door behind him. His car spun around; as it picked up speed he disposed of me with a careless wave of his hand. Wheels showering the roadside with mud, the command car pivoted and followed. The police wagon maneuvered strenuously until it, too, headed the other way. Now I caught my first view of the Arab prisoner. Tired and haggard-looking, he stared out at the receding land- scape. I noticed Tamar; her eyes were fixed on the same stark shape, growing distant inside the green car. Absent-mindedly, she came and stood beside me. "It must be the infiltrator," I said. My uncertainty won her confidence. It proved that I, too, was an outsider. "What can he be thinking?" she asked, averting her glance from me. "That they're taking him back to jail . . ?"

We were still talking when the police wagon stopped short with an unnerving suddenness that was almost comic. At first nothing happened. Then a door slammed, tires squealed and the car sped off again, leaving an old man behind on the road. He came toward us, hunched beneath a dark raincoat and crumpled hat. I knew at once who he was and I pictured to myself the scene which must have taken place in the front seat when the old man, realizing belatedly that they were leaving, that they might be gone for an hour, had demanded that they stop and let him off. He headed straight for the van, which was now the only shelter against the wind and rain. I lost sight of him and noticed that Tamar had again gone off toward the border. They should both be put in the driver's cabin, I thought, but one look in that direction was enough to change my mind. The morning paper had disappeared; in its place, sporting a handsome beard, sat a pale-faced young rabbi who had been assigned to accompany the corpses.

Gusts of wind drove thick sheets of rain across the road. I motioned the girl to climb into the van. If her duty was to wait for her sister, mine was to see that she at least acted sensibly. But she gave no indication of having understood. She seemed lost in herself as I approached, yet was not startled when I brushed her wet sleeve.

"Get inside! Hurry up!"

"Thanks. I'd rather not."

"Save your thanks. You have to. Hurry up!"

"I don't want to." It went on stupidly for a few minutes. Finally, I threatened her: "I'll call the officer and we'll make you get inside."

"Do you know who I am?" she asked suddenly, returning the threat.

"Certainly I know. But that has nothing to do with standing in the rain." I grabbed her by the arm and pulled. Her obstinacy had led me to expect more of a fight, but she let herself be dragged along easily, submissively. When we got to the truck, however, she stiffened and balked.

"What's the matter?"

"You mustn't tell him who I am."

"Tell who?"

"The old man. Doctor Chafetz."

I hadn't realized that he was a doctor or that he didn't know who she was. The question troubled me: Why didn't he know? Why mustn't he be told? But, since to wait for an answer meant standing with her in the rain, I nodded my silent consent. She didn't need any help, but I boosted her onto the platform of the truck, jumped in after her, and slid the wooden bench around from its place by the wall. She chose to sit at the back of the truck next to the tarpaulin, where she was hidden from the old man's sight.

The old man's broad-brimmed, shapeless gray fedora lay on his matted hair as if it had been dropped from above and was too small for such a head: unruly white shocks protruded from beneath it in all directions. The bench rattled under us as we sat. His quiet, blue stare came to rest on me, the eyes marked by deep wrinkles. He was ill at ease. Removing his glasses, he shut his eyes and polished the lenses slowly and carefully. When they were bright and shiny he replaced them deliberately, and asked, so abruptly that I was taken aback, "May I presume you, then, to be the relations?"

He was alluding to us both, and I more than kept my word to Tamar by answering "No." "My son," he said, gesturing vaguely toward the Hebron hills, "Yehoyariv. Yehoyariv Chafetz. I am among the relations requested to appear for the identification. If you will pardon a trite phrase, there yet remains a shadow of doubt and, truthfully, I ask myself whether his name has not been mistaken for someone else's. The fact of the matter is, he went to the Galilee. The girl's relations . . ." he broke off uncertainly ". . . . not one of them has come?" He looked at me, then stared at the girl, studying her hair and shoulders. Like most old teachers who have lectured a great deal, he made little distinction between a question and a statement of fact, talking as if to himself, sometimes pausing to reflect, sometimes challenging his own assertions. His voice was quite pleasant, unhurried and inoffensive. But behind that exterior, it seemed to me, a mind schooled in abstractions was racing madly to protect itself against naked reality. Beyond the façade of hair and shoulders to my right, I could sense the fear-glazed eyes of the girl staring into the rain, all too aware of the truth.

"And you, sir, if I may be permitted to ask, who are you?" The question gave me a start, though the style of delivery was by now familiar; clearly, this was how he addressed his students. "I'm from the government," I said, suddenly content with the small, honest affirmation.

"The government." He broke the word into syllables,

as if demonstrating its pronunciation. "In that case, perhaps you know for what purpose we are being kept waiting?"

"I don't suppose it depends on us," I said.

"But on some other government," said the old man, filling out the sentence to suit himself. "The Lord be praised, every people has its government. Or on the rain." He talked into the gloomy shelter, which grew murkier as the sky outside darkened and the front windshield fogged over. "The night rains," he continued, "can wash out all the roads below Hebron. The Hebron-Beersheba road runs, does it not, through the center of the southernmost portion of the Hebron basin, in distinction to its northern counterparts, which all face in a westerly direction. On its way to the Basor this basin amasses huge quantities of run-off, coming from two divides, the Artzit, and the one between the Shikma and the Basor. We should not forget that near Hebron are two isohyetic areas of eight hundred millimeters each. One night of solid rain isolates the villagers on Mount Hebron, and delays all traffic to Beersheba by half a day at the very least. Flash floods . . ."

The old man had a tendency to ramble on. Piqued by the girl's presence, he sought to gain her attention, in such a way that her stubborn silence, too, became part of the conversation. A professional vice, I thought to myself, at the same time trying to read something of her mind. "When will he shut up," she seemed to be thinking. "Who can listen to all these lectures?"

"Since you seem unable to enlighten me in regard to the present and why we are waiting here, certainly you will be equally at a loss in regard to the future and how long we shall have to wait. Perhaps, however, you are in a position to shed some light on the past. Quite frankly, I know less than nothing." Without waiting for

183

an answer, he continued. "Yesterday evening there was a knock on the door. 'Does Yehuda Chafetz live here?' The policeman confused the name. 'Yehoyariv Chafetz,' I said. 'What is the matter?' The policeman didn't know, he was only sent to inquire whether Yehoyariv was at home, and if not, where was he. Shortly after he left, someone more important came, an officer. He went over each question again, as if nobody had been there before him. Since then I have repeated my story countless times, but like water poured upon sand it falls on deaf ears. To be sure, my son Yehoyariv left a week ago, but his travels led him northward, to the Galilee. To the best of my knowledge, in his own words—which were always precisely chosen —his plan was to tour the Galilee, starting from the Valley of Genosar and working northward through Migdal to Nahal Amud, in order to make a survey of the plant life there. We have a journal called *Land and Nature* and our correspondent in the Galilee was to go with him, our correspondent on weather, nature, geographical data of all sorts . . ."

The girl's shoes scraped against the metal bumper at the rear. She barely raised herself from her sitting position, and slid outside, feet first. The old man was upset. "Has anything happened?" A car was approaching from the direction of Beersheba. "Perhaps the relations have arrived," he said, glancing first outside and then back at me, as if to appeal to my better judgment. As before, he did not wait for an answer. "We didn't know her. Not even by name. We only knew her address at the district school, and her initials, M.G.D., short for Migdalit, which is how she signed those articles of hers, so terse and lucid. We knew she was a school-teacher, we thought she must be shy. Even if I could be led to believe that my son might have reversed his direction and gone south to the Judean hills, crossing through Jordan from Hartuv to Ein Gedi, still it violates all logic to suppose that she . . . that it's possible . . ."

His hands, which had been clasped between his knees, spread apart tremulously, palms upward, to express his bewilderment. The words he added were quite unnecessary. "I don't understand, it makes no sense, I simply refuse to believe . . ."

Two sisters, I thought. Both schoolteachers. One is successful, talented, writes articles. The boy from the Capital asks her to come camping and exploring. The other is jealous, she tries to tag along. They give her the slip. Instead of going north, they head south. It's obvious, I thought. She must feel guilt-stricken.

The army rabbi approached from behind, surveyed us both, and addressed himself to me. "Bread and tea have arrived, if you want any." I brought the old man some tea in a flat military bowl, and thick slices of bread and sardines. He placed the bread beside him on the bench and buried his face in the tea, tilting his head slowly backward until he had gulped it all down. He laid the bowl down by the bread and stared outside. The storm had lifted and the sky was clearing. "The relations, then, have not arrived?" He had found his tongue again. "We didn't know if she had any relations, and if she did, whether they were parents, sisters, brothers . . . We never knew. We only corresponded, and of late it was Yehoyariv who undertook this. In his last letter he wrote: 'I should like to catalogue the flowers and plants of the Galilee.' As usual, she answered punctually, 'Let's go together.' And they went . . ."

When I returned the empty bowl I inquired whether the girl had drunk anything. "What girl?" I was asked. She was standing by the border sign again. They filled

185

a bowl of tea for her, and after thinking it over, I made do with that. If she wants to eat she can come over here. I brought her the bowl without spilling a drop; the air was still damp, but the thick liquid surface of the tea was unruffled. She accepted it silently and took two careful sips.

"What are you staring at?"

"You can have something to eat if you want," I said.

"Who asked you to look after me?"

I reached for a cigarette, my first since leaving Joe's car.

"Smoke?"

"No," she said; all her feelings toward me were bound up in that one word. I smoked in silence, making it clear that I was only waiting to return the empty bowl. "Go to the old man. You'd better look after him."

"He asked about you again," I replied gingerly, "about the relations. He talked a lot about your sister. With great respect."

"He's never even seen her, how can he talk about her?" She had been gazing down at the road, at the wet, cracked asphalt and the muddied patterns. Now she shot me a wild, quick glance. "Take your tea. Get out of here!" She flung the bowl onto the pavement and it rolled about clattering on the ground. She ran after it immediately, bent over, picked it up, and handed it back to me. "What do you want? What business is it of yours? Who asked you to get mixed up in this?"

I crushed the cigarette under my heel and turned to go, gripping the bowl in my hand. It's all right, I thought, it's understandable.

I returned the bowl to one of the soldiers, who tossed it over his shoulder into the open compartment. The old man sat in the van chewing on a piece of bread, the bearded rabbi beside him. He stopped when he saw me and motioned me over with his hand, searching for an opening word. "I beg of you," he said, gesturing with his bread toward the rabbi. "Observe what these gentlemen have been saying. The dead girl was apparently a soldier. From the army. So you see, it can't be our couple after all . . ."

"Can't you leave him alone for a while?" I asked the rabbi angrily. I didn't like him, and now that I felt responsible for the two of them, I couldn't stand the way he picked at their wounds, first feeding the old man all sorts of stories, then scolding him for being confused.

"He thought I was one of the relatives," the rabbi said, jumping to the ground. My manner had convinced him that I was important, and he followed me obsequiously across the road, tendering apologies. "He asked me, am I related, so I said I'm a chaplain and he asked what's a chaplain. I explained to him . . . the burial unit . . . when a soldier gets killed. He said my son isn't a soldier. So I told him it's a girl, that's all I know, and he kept asking me questions . . ."

It was nearly eight o'clock. Slowly, the sky began to brighten. The convoy returned: first the police wagon, then Joe's sedan and the staff car filled with soldiers.

"They're coming!" someone yelled, pointing up the road toward Hebron.

In the distance we made out the white cars of the U.N., and Arab Legion jeeps escorting a truck. "Well," said Joe, "this is it. Who's coming with me?"

Accompanied by a staff Major we advanced past the sign. Where the road dipped lay the border, sealed by steel spikes heavily laced with barbed wire. Fifty meters further off was a second roadblock, theirs, where men were working to clear a path. Halfway between the two barriers, beside an open car, U.N. officials and Legion officers waited with their credentials. An amiable French

Colonel presided correctly over handshakes and salutes, and apologized for the delay.

"Of course," I said. "The rain. Flash floods . . ."

"But yes," he said, pleasantly surprised. "How did monsieur know?"

He spoke to his chauffeur, who reached into a hand-tooled liquor cabinet and brought out several glasses. The Colonel filled them himself, telling us about the floods, which were so bad that they had to wait for the water to drain off the roads and bridges. "But not a drop got into the brandy," Joe quipped, and the Colonel laughed heartily. I gladly accepted a second glass.

"Would you like to see them?" the Colonel asked.

"No," said Joe, "the next of kin have been waiting for hours."

The Legionaires expressed their sympathy. The Colonel corked the bottle and handed it back. The chauffeur collected the empty glasses. The Legion officers saluted and left. We remained behind by the car. "Send blankets with the stretchers," the Colonel advised, ignoring our parting handshakes and walking alongside us. The glasses tinkled as they went back into the cabinet. "The black devils wouldn't even let us have a closed truck," he confided. "I argued with them for an hour. They said that on rainy days only open trucks were available. I wanted you to see them before the next of kin . . . very well, send dry blankets . . . the blankets on them now are soaked through."

The Major volunteered to see to it. He saluted and strode quickly back towards our lines. We followed behind.

At the border the Colonel took Joe's hand in his own, detaining him for a brief moment. "She was one of the loveliest girls I have ever seen in this land, and I am not one to go about with my eyes shut. She could not have been more than eighteen." He spoke gently, with compassion.

"Nineteen," Joe said.

"A fine fellow," he said to me, once we had recrossed the barrier and slowly climbed the hill. "A good friend and a good drinking companion—and once even a good soldier."

"According to the old man," I replied, groping for what was baffling me, "I had the impression that she was at least twenty-five."

"What does he know about it, the old man? He doesn't even know her name . . ."

I flushed with surprise, as if the two glasses of brandy had gone to my head.

"But he knew that she taught school, she wrote nature columns for his journal. It's not in character for a nineteen-year-old girl . . ."

"So he confused you too? The poor fellow. It's Tamar here who's the teacher, the sister . . ."

"But . . ." I didn't finish, perhaps because there was something I wanted to know which even Joe didn't know.

"But what?" he asked, half indifferently. I didn't answer. Still I needed to be sure. "Perhaps they were both teachers?"

"Ziva Tshernobilsky was in a Nahal Brigade," said Joe, closing the argument. "She belonged to a unit at Ein Gedi. A short furlough home—then she decided to hike back, by the direct route across Jordan. She took her boyfriend along . . ."

Hers or her sister's? I nodded automatically, but I no longer heard what Joe was saying. God forgive me, I felt happy inside. Something was approaching fulfillment. With a cool, imperturbable desire, I wanted Tamar to know that I, and only I, shared her secret.

I bided my time. At the top of the hill Joe grew philosophical. "There's really nothing left for me to do here. Two long funerals now, and then it's over."

At the signpost we came across the old man. Craning his neck, he licked his dry lips without daring to speak. But he couldn't restrain himself entirely. "What," he asked, "what? Are we going for them? Not yet?" We stopped beside him.

"Soon," Joe said, and added encouragingly: "But we needn't go ourselves. The police will bring them." His words were inadequate, but he was afraid to say more; anything else would have been just as bad.

A column swung by, four soldiers led by an officer, with two policemen carrying folded stretchers and blankets over their shoulders. They marched forward, then halted at an outcry from below in English and Arabic. "Only the police!" yelled Joe, running after them. "Only the police with the stretchers. The army isn't allowed here. A demilitarized zone . . ." I had to strain to catch his last words. The soldiers returned; the police hesitated, then started out again. The old man fidgeted. He wouldn't let them out of his sight. Each time I tried to restrain him he squirmed loose and trotted after them. The stretchers spoke a language which he finally understood. At a vantage point overlooking the scene below, we caught up with Joe.

Two U.N. officials, their dress uniforms gleaming in a sudden burst of sunlight, stepped forward to help the stretcher-bearers. The stretchers were extended full-length now, although still empty. They advanced toward the Jordanian ranks, and the old man trembled as they disappeared among them. Joe tried to calm him: "They'll be back in a jiffy. Soon they'll bring them." He stared back uncomprehendingly, unable to decide which of us had spoken. "It makes no sense," he mumbled, "none, none at all. At this very moment they are somewhere in the Galilee. It is inconceivable that they should have forgotten the December issue. It was to be specially devoted to our Galilean flora. And she said they would go together, she wrote him, 'I'll take three days off from my teaching' . . ."

The truth was right under Joe's nose, and I stole a glance at him, suspecting that now he would grasp it. He raised his eyebrows at me over the old man's shoulders: "Didn't I tell you—he's out of his mind." I nearly laughed out loud.

"Here they come!" I cried exultantly, and was immediately ashamed of myself. They came in twos, walking slowly and with difficulty, carrying one stretcher after another. The rabbi appeared at our side, his face sweet and composed, fingering the book which he held in his hands. He opened it to the correct place, smoothed out the page, and then closed it, using his finger as a placemark. Obviously, he was a man of some experience. When the stretchers passed the second roadblock he opened the book again and began reading silently to himself.

"Are you a relation?" the old man asked him, his eyes on the book.

"I've already told you, from the army," whispered the rabbi, "on a military assignment, the Lord is my Rock and my Fortress." He stood chanting at the approaching stretchers.

"You, sir, are a relation!" The old man held on to me in a daze, tremors passing from his body into mine. "You have no right to conceal the facts from me any longer. How could it be, it's not possible, through what error could they have come here, my son and your good daughter . . ." He may have been angry or simply bewildered. Torn between pity and apprehension myself, I pulled him closer, keeping my footing and managing to support him at the same time. Joe must have thought I was squeamish; this time I was sure he would suspect something, but he was too busy with the stretchers to notice either of us. The old man, too, loosened his grip and watched with rapt attention. The stretchers sagged heavily beneath the weight of the bodies, swaying perceptibly despite the bearers' efforts to keep them straight. On the steep grade the bodies jiggled and slid back. The corner of a blanket hung down from the second stretcher and a naked foot flashed whitely. They passed before us in a miniature procession. The rabbi, the old man and I joined it at the rear.

Following Joe's directions, the driver skillfully maneuvered the van until its back faced us. Joe and his crew stepped aside, the rear flap was opened noisily, and the stretchers were brought into position. The end of the first stretcher was heaved onto the truck; one of the bearers jumped onto the platform and pulled at it from inside, while another continued to push. Then, the second stretcher. The old man came forward, stopped, rested his elbows on the floor and buried his head in his hands. Beneath the blankets, the two bodies were indistinguishably alike: a head, knees, hands and feet. "It's impossible," he said, and nobody heard him. "I can't, I can't . . ."

The U.N. officials smoothed the creases out of their jackets and surreptitiously rubbed their hands, which were numb from exertion. There was an awkward moment of indecision, of covert glances. By the time Joe realized that the old man would not be able to go through with it, it was too late to have the stretchers lowered again. "Where's the girl?" he asked. "Here!" She was right behind us. "Put him in the cabin." The driver and the rabbi led the old man away. He was weeping uncontrollably.

"I can manage by myself," Tamar said, when Joe and I tried to help her up. She moved forward two steps, knelt on one knee by the corpse on the left, raised the corner of the blanket ever so slightly, then immediately laid it back in place. Motionless, she choked back a cry. Her other knee sank to the floor.

"I was absolutely certain," whispered Joe.

She straightened up slightly and turned to the stretcher on the right. This time she raised the corner of the blanket and held it a long while, straining to absorb all she could in the dim light. "What's going on there?" Joe whispered. "Have you any doubts?" he demanded of her. Frightened, she dropped the blanket and lifted her face towards us, her eyes shut against the sunlight. She half rose and moved heavily toward the back of the van, avoiding us with her eyes. "What doubts? I never even saw him."

"Good enough," said Joe, "We'll finish up in Beer-sheba. Close the door. Let's get going." Silently, Tamar let me help her down. We heard the door slam shut. Joe was already somewhere else, but she continued to answer his question anyway. "They arrived in our village together, by accident, on the ten o'clock bus. She was on leave from the army, he had come from Jerusalem . . ."

From beyond the van a detachment of police brought forward the infiltrator; afraid to outdistance his escort, he waited after every order to make sure it was all right to go on. Joe directed the operation from behind. "Let him go," he said in Hebrew, and then, to the two U.N. officials in French: "Everything is in order. You may take him."

"I had made all the necessary preparations for the

three days I would be away. At eleven I left the school. Mother and Father were out in the orchard."

The Arab walked north between them like a sentenced man, hugging his arms close to his body as if they were still in chains. His fear had yet to wear off.

"She left a note, and her uniform, and they were gone before any of us came back. They went straight down the road, to the south . . ."

—*Translated by Hillel Halkin*

YEHUDA AMIHAI

Battle
for
the
Hill

Yehuda Amihai, born in Germany in 1924, has lived in Israel since the age of twelve. During the Second World War he enlisted in the British army and served four years in the Middle East, after which he joined the Palmach, the shock troops of the Israeli army. Following the War of Independence, Amihai studied at the Hebrew University. After a year abroad in England and the United States, he returned to Jerusalem to teach in one of the city's high schools.

Amihai began publishing poetry in the early nineteen-fifties. Two volumes of his verse have appeared so far: Achshav U'vyamin Aherim *("Now and in Other Days,"* 1955) *and* Bemerhak Shtey Tikvot *("At a Distance of Two Hopes,"* 1958). *The present story is taken from a collection of the writer's short stories,* Baruah Hanora'ah Hazot *("In This Terrible Wind"), published in* 1961. *"Battle for the Hill" is set in Jerusalem during the Sinai Campaign of 1956, when the city, protected by thousands of suddenly mobilized citizen-soldiers, waited five long days for a war which never came. The title is itself an ironic comment on the countless war stories with similar names which have filled Israel's periodicals during the past two decades.*

My wife and I crossed the street which led to where our friends live. We passed by the leper hospital, but as usual I failed to see a single one of the white invalids among the old trees. You never see them. The gates are always open, footsteps have trodden the grass and wheels have flattened it, but one never sees a soul. Sometimes you see milk cans standing before one of the iron doors sunk deep within the wall. I have yet to see a milkman.

One day last winter I stood beside this same wall and took refuge from a sudden cloudburst. I stood under the small corrugated roof which projects from it at an angle. I have no idea why the slanting roof was built. I stood fixed beneath it like a holy icon in some Christian land. Standing there, I watched the last fugitives fleeing from the rain and listened to the noise they made as they splashed through the puddles.

Now, however, a soldier stood near the wall. I watched him gesture with his hands as if he were directing traffic. There were no cars within sight or hearing, but I spotted a young woman crossing a field covered with rocks and briars. The soldier motioned to her with his hands, and I heard him call out: "More to the right, that's it, and now to the left again. No, no! Not towards me. Away from me. That's right, that's right." The woman obeyed his directions, growing smaller until she disappeared; I doubt if she will ever see him again, or if he will see her.

Our friends live on a plot of land which is not .theirs and in a house which is not theirs. The armchair in the living room has finally been repaired, and the bay window is at rest at last. It is recessed and placid, like a gulf into which ships no longer venture. For the first time in years the iron gate was open. The wash was hung out to dry; shirts and pants swayed freed of the body, like our thoughts, which are formed in our bodies but sometimes fly free in the wind. My friend's wife runs a kindergarten. The front yard contained a playground: a slide and a tiny ladder for make-believe angels. The children push and shove each other until they reach the top. The pleasure of sliding down lasts no longer than a second. A small boy, who seemed to have been forgotten from the day before, stood there holding a red balloon in his hands. An old car, stripped of its wheels and motor and painted red, rested in the sand for the children to play with. In a like manner the ideas of my forefathers have come down to me: just the frame with a bright coat of paint. Sometimes it seems that I sit in them, or play with them, but I never go anywhere.

The army runner came looking for me. The same soldier I had seen giving directions to his wife turned out to be the runner of my company, who had been dispatched to bring me in. He is always on the run, with some message in his hand or mouth. Now I spied him coming down the walled-in road. A piece of white paper fluttered in his hands like a captured butterfly. He caught up with me as I stood in the playground beside the painted car. Gasping and panting he halted before me short of breath, looking the way runners are supposed to look. I read what was written on the paper. Instead of going on to see our friends, I sat my wife down in the sand box next to the forgotten boy, and proceeded to the mobilization room at the army base. I passed through many rooms: the buffet, the engineering corps room, the synagogue, the quartermaster's room, the bathroom—until finally I came to the mobilization room. There I expected to find a great bustle of people, coming and going in a hurry, but I found only two women soldiers sitting in front of the door. "Wait just a minute!" they said in unison as I approached, and then settled down again. One of them wore a blouse with a flower pattern and a khaki skirt, the other a khaki blouse and a skirt with a flower pattern—like clowns at Purim. It had all happened suddenly. One of them had been on leave and had just had time to put on her khaki blouse again when there came a knock on her front door. The other was preparing to go on leave and had already removed her army skirt when they knocked on *her* door. In the confusion she had snatched the skirt with the flower pattern that was draped over the back of a chair, and had put it on, holding it tight with both hands because she couldn't find the zipper.

"We weren't expecting this."

"We weren't ready."

"Can I go in now?"

"One moment. What's the rush? You'll get there."

"We weren't ready. It happened so suddenly."

"It always comes suddenly."

"The bottom of your slip is showing."

"I know. It's too long for the khaki skirt."

"When I'm in uniform, I don't wear my slip."

"Too bad."

"We just weren't ready."

Then I heard the sound of chairs being moved about inside the room. Distant doors opened and slammed shut, and heavy footsteps resounded through the building.

"You can enter now. Come in!" said a voice from within.

It was getting on towards evening. The last rays of sunshine slanted through the drawn blinds, staining my forehead with a golden light. I wiped the stains from my forehead like beads of sweat, and entered. My captain sat at the table and did not bother to turn around. He was surrounded by maps on every side. On one of them lay a pair of eyeglasses. A second pair he wore. I have never been able to make up my mind whether I like him or hate him. Watching him once during target practice, I saw him remove his glasses, and noticed that there was sadness in his eyes. Ever since then he has risen in my esteem. Now he continued to bend over the table, still without turning around. Like the Roman god Janus, he had two faces. Bristling with tiny hairs and unaware of the future, the expressionless face of his neck looked towards me, while the face which had eyes and a nose looked towards the map. It is my belief that if there is an end to this universe and if there is a God, there is also a gigantic neck, the face of which looks out towards the space beyond and is never seen. The captain's neck said to me:

"Sit down, sit down. I'll be with you in a minute."

"I left my wife in the sand box."

"You did well."

"By the monkey bars and the slide. The tea will get cold."

"Come have a look at the photograph."

I came closer but saw nothing. I held the dark paper up against the evening light and saw that it was an X-ray. They had taken an X-ray of the entire location and of the hill. A strange bone had gotten into it, however, and I saw all my sadness and the negative of my white wife sitting in the sand box beneath the clothesline. A breeze sprang up and papers rustled and fell to the floor. Tea was brought, and I placed my glass upon the map. "The tea is exactly over the objective," said my captain. "The point we have to capture is underneath your glass."

Afterwards he entrusted me with a list of the names

of those who had to be assembled. "You have to tell them when to leave their homes. Synchronize your watch with mine. You have to begin everything from the end. In reverse. But to return to the present moment, perhaps one should draw up the battle order to cover the past too, as far back as kindergarten: the attack, the final preparations, the good-by to the wife, the last kiss, inspection of the boots, the next to the last good-by; hopes and delusions; "relative" peace, marriage, study, a course in communications and breaking of communications, a course in love and disappointment, father dies in the night, school, kindergarten; there you have your battle order and the calendar in reverse," laughed my captain. We stood by the window, and he rested his arm on my shoulder. "In retrospect, in retrospect," he said. . . .

I went to the buffet; my wife sat in the corner over a glass of yellow juice, a straw in her mouth. She did not drink; rather, the glass seemed to drink her. As on those moonlit nights, when she grows diffuse and becomes sad and empty and cannot sleep, I held on to the back of her hands, which held on to the cold glass. The small, lithe girls, wriggling in their dresses behind the counter, signaled to me that they wished to close the room for the night. The room will be closed. The world will be closed. The buffet will grow dark; the world will grow dark. As soon as my wife fell asleep I rose to my feet and left. From here on we shall grow accustomed to strange good-bys. By the glass, by the white pillow, by the door and by all the other strange places. They are lucky, these soldiers who are shipped across the great sea; the awful ripping of paper in every good-by is swallowed by the tremulous onrush of the waves. Here a great noise is needed to still the voice of my wife in the house next door, behind the front line.

My life has always been either the noise before the stillness or the stillness before the noise. Between them I can get no rest. Will it be noisy or still, I wonder, when death comes to take me? . . .

The company clerk came and handed me the mobilization slips, as if it were a lottery. I went about the city, waking my friends so that they might gird themselves for battle. It was not always easy to do this by myself. Later I lost a number of my men. I distributed the white slips. Some were crammed through cracks in the doors like whispering snakes. Children babbled in their sleep. I answered them wakefully and they lapsed into silence. Cars cruised quietly by, secretly sliding around corners. Grown men cried. The eucalyptus tree had insomnia; it shook all over. Each leaf was an open, smarting eye. One day, when there is peace, I shall place a eucalyptus branch where my heavy heart now lies. I stretched my hand into no-man's land and touched a piece of paper thrown by the enemy. A midnight wind blew through the fragments of bottles. To confuse the enemy I sped to the other end of town. A woman stood in a doorway in a vacant lot and said, "He's not home, he's not home!" I heard the water being flushed in the bathroom; her husband emerged drunk with sleep, following after me as in the tale of the golden goose: whoever touches its feathers is caught fast, and must go along with it, no matter what.

I turned off my flashlight; the beam returned like a well-trained dog. We descended to the cellar, where the smell of poverty and children's sleep greeted my nostrils. But my friend was already standing before me in uniform, his pack slung over his shoulder. "What do you have in that pack?" "I don't know." His forehead was pale and deeply lined, like stairs which have been walked on a great deal. His wife stood behind me dressed in a billowy white robe. "Don't mind her," he said. She is dying already, and every evening at midnight she will appear to him. The woman faded from sight, and in her place came the steps, as white as she had been.

The roosters cry all through the night, not only at dawn. I cannot sleep the whole night long and during the day I dream. Dreams hovered above the city like vapor from a hot drink. Water flowed through every drainpipe on every roof. A single car shot off in several directions. Like my head: only my mouth remained stationary and refused to run about as did the other parts of my face. Men received instructions like police cars and shifted direction. I slipped away from the soldiers who were rounding up the company, and went off to the buffet to fetch my wife. I woke the officer on duty. Sleeping soldiers littered the lawns and footpaths. I opened the door of the buffet. My wife was slumped over a tabletop, sticky with old candy, still gripping her glass. I picked her up, the glass clutched in her hand. Light struck it and it shimmered. On the way out my wife slipped from my grasp and fell, breaking the glass. My wife banged her head. She didn't even groan, and I became frightened. We sat together by the roadside. You could hear the frog-talk over the wireless in the radio car. I carried my wife home and put her to bed.

"Did you pick up the broken glass?"

"I picked it up and now I have to go."

"Why? Where to?"

"I took it you knew."

"Once you said 'I take you to be my wedded wife,' and we broke a glass then too."

"Once we sat by a white wall with vines on it."

"My head hurts."

"Because you fell. Soon it will be dawn. Do you hear a car?"

"Yes."

"They're coming for me."

"No, it's the milkman."

"No, it's the army car that's coming for me."

I packed my shirts and a few pairs of underwear. The time I had allotted to myself was up. The vehicle which passed was not the milk truck, and it was not for me. I took my belongings. When I opened my neatly pressed white handkerchief to wipe my brow, I saw that printed upon it was a plan of the enemy hill: a lonely tumble-down shack, and next to it a number of well-fortified positions. My name was embroidered below: the first initials of my name in the corner of the handkerchief which bore the plan. The approaches were indicated by arrows, the artillery emplacement by crosses or circles. I folded the handkerchief without wiping my brow. I saw that my wife was sleeping. I saw the pieces of broken glass in the street and went out. On the stairway, I switched on the light to look at the handkerchief again. What was the hill called? From where would we attack? How would we set up the light machine guns, and where would we evacuate the wounded and through what conduit in the world would all the blood flow? The long-destined hill. The ultimate hill. I have heard that the sun rises in the East. I heard the first pedestrians in the streets and I hoped that my wife would sleep on and on. I folded the handkerchief lovingly and put it away. I drank a cup of coffee standing up, without sensing the taste of war. New death notices had been put up on the bulletin board. There were also posters calling on the residents of different cities to assemble for memorial rallies in honor of the six million. In all probability these were mobilization calls in disguise. The newspaper fell from my hands and I let it lie.

A car drove up and stopped near me: "Come with me." "Where are you going? You're not from the army?" The driver laughed and said, "Don't you see the way I've smeared the windshields with mud?" The earth is rising. The fragrance of the earth is rising. He then showed me pictures of his children. "Where are we going?" He held his hand up before my eyes and said, "Here is the map, we will follow the lines on my palm." The water swashed about in his canteen. "Soon we will be home again," I said to calm him. Like my mother, who used to calm us by saying about everything that it was nothing. If it was blistering hot she said, "Just another summer day." When it hailed she said, "How pleasant the air is, so mild and fresh! It's good that it's not too dry. It's good there is no drought."

The strings from which I dangled like a marionette in a puppet show became entwined and tangled among other strings; when somebody else was supposed to move I moved instead, and vice versa. And all the time the voice fixed above our heads continued to talk. I asked the driver to stop, and I went to call one of the men in my company who lived in a large courtyard; the passageway was still sealed off with the branches of trees that had broken during the winter. Over the door was a sheet of paper with the names of all the tenants. Next to each name was written how many times to ring. I rang four times. I waited, but the door did not open. I watched the open army trucks pass by, decked out with the long hair of girls, with antennas and machine guns. Although I knew that there was still time, I hid behind the door. I heard footsteps approaching. The door opened. A man saw me and turned pale; he then returned to his room to put on his glasses. Then

he begged my pardon for the delay in opening the door;
he didn't know if it was ringing for him. Sometimes it
rings four times and it's not for him. During his vaca-
tions he lies on his back and counts the number of
rings. He is always waiting. He has often been mistaken. He has often been mistaken in his life. He is a
teacher and there are stacks of notebooks in his room,
filled with red marks correcting students' mistakes. Like
his life. In his room is a single window, and the blinds
are generally lowered. He finished arranging his things
and came with me. Civilian cars which had been com-
mandeered for the war passed by, camouflaged with
mud and dark blankets.

Towards evening I was assigned to observe the hill
with the shack for the first time. I entered a house which
stood near the border. The stairway was empty and the
plaster was peeling from the walls, on which a few
mailboxes hung. In one box the letters overflowed. The
tenant was long gone, but the letters continued to arrive. Sometimes, when I have wandered far in my
thoughts, people speak to me and their words clutter
the gateways to my being without penetrating any
further, because I do not choose to admit them.

I went up to the top floor. A woman wiping her hands
on an apron let me in. I showed her the letter from the
army. Domestic odors permeated the house. A pressure
burner chattered noisily. A girl sang in the bathtub and
soap bubbles popped all over her—but I was unable to
see. My heart welled up within me, and all the words
which had accumulated in my head like letters in the
abandoned mail box suddenly fell and glutted my heart
instead. I recalled my mission and my eyes grew bleary
with worry, like the camouflaged windshields which
were smeared with mud. A boy stood and stared at me.
I formed an arch over him like the vault of the skies;

the worries smudged my eyes. The boy's mouth was smudged with food. I ascended to the attic. I lay down between the wooden crates with the boy at my feet. "What are you looking at?" he asked. "At the years to come," I answered, "and at my wife lying in bed because her head is broken." The boy left; I heard his laugh from a distance. My captain was already at the window. The wire screen was in our way. We ripped it apart and were deluged by dust. My captain passed me the binoculars.

"Do you see that ridge? Do you see that line, that elevation, that trench, that point?" I saw them, and we compared them with the map. The world was exact and efficient. My captain got up to go. "Stay a while," he said to me, "and take notes on whatever you see." I took notes: A man went by with his donkey. A man went by with his wife. The sun is slowly setting. A man is stretching himself by the shack and lifting his two arms. To whom is he surrendering?

I heard footsteps behind me. The boy returned and began to ask questions. I gave him pencil and paper and told him to draw the hill. He drew the hill with himself standing on it. He drew a flag and a ball rolling down the slope. More officers arrived to take their first glimpse of the lonely outpost. I returned by way of the apartment. The bathroom door was open and the burner had stopped chattering. I asked permission to wash my hands. The girl whose voice I had heard before stood in front of me. "Why are you staring at me like a dummy?" she said. "Help me dry my back!" I took the towel and massaged her skin until it turned red.

"What did you do up there in the attic?" she asked.

"We looked."

"Did you see my old dolls?"

"I'll come back."

"My back is already dry. Now on your way!"

She laughed, tossing her thick black hair. Her eyes sparkled and her mouth was red. Drops of water from her hair fell onto my khaki shirt and dried instantly. Her snub nose was fresh and provoking. She caught me by the ears and said, "You're coming back, you're coming back to me!" After seeing her, I couldn't go straight back to the army, so I took a roundabout route by way of the valleys which encircle the city. The Spanish consul drove past in his automobile. The consul of chaos hoisted his ensign. Jews gathered in the Orthodox quarter of Mea Shearim to cry "Ma'ariv Ma'ariv,"* their faces turned toward an east which is no longer the East. East is the magnetic pole of the Jews. I glanced at my watch and saw that it was time to be in the school building for the parents' meeting; I sat in the teachers' lounge and waited for the parents to arrive. Whatever way you look at it, there is no helping the parents and no preventing bloodshed on the hill with the shack. Only time can occasionally intervene and permit life to linger on a little longer. Bergman stuck his head in the door to see if I had come. One of his children is alive and the other is dead. The dead child is lobbying for him in the world to come. He has already made inroads among the dead; he is an honorary consul in heaven. The child who is still living studies with me. Bergman was with me in the army during the Second World War. Now he sat silently before me. In the glass cabinet there stood the physics apparatus: pieces that interlock, for example, though we never interlock; or the lead ball, which after being heated cannot pass through the ring because it no longer fits. There were also shells from Elath in which you could listen to the

* "Ma'ariv" is the Jewish daily evening prayer. Literally, the word means "evening," and is related to the word "ma'arav," which means "west."

sea, and a paper world glued to a globe, very like the world glued to the head on my shoulders, which is also nearly round.

The sister of one of my pupils approached me; she was already grown up and married. One of her eyes she fixed on me; the other was blind and white, with the eyeball turned inward. Aging fathers came who failed to recognize their own sons: "Which one do you mean, which one do you mean, Yosef or Shmuel?" Fathers resemble their sons and everybody resembles everybody, and we are all enemies nonetheless. I placed the plan of the hill beside my grade book, and from time to time I peeked at it. Beneath the grades for discipline, for good behavior and arithmetic, were the dotted lines which stood for the enemy positions. I had been informed that my company was not to be held responsible for capturing the entire hill, but only for its southern slope. Beyond that there remained a few dirt embankments, and a handful of enemy soldiers sitting behind them. When we really attack it will not be necessary to pin numbers on our backs like basketball players to avoid mistaking one side for the other; we won't make mistakes. And if we do, that too is ultimately no mistake. In the meantime much was happening: The sun set. Children screamed. A wind blew. Dust came and the window was shut. As in the Book of Job, one messenger was followed by another. The teacher, Miss Ziva, had arrived.

"We're on to you, we know all about you."

I covered the plan with my hand so that Ziva should not see it. It was forbidden for security reasons.

"We know all about you, all about the girl whose back you wiped."

Miss Ziva has read widely and is an expert on weather conditions and the heavenly winds. She is prettier in winter than in summer. Someone's father stepped forward and complained that his son was noisy and unruly, that he colored the walls of the house all the colors of the sunset, that he threw stones at cats and dogs and was spoiling his mother's dreams.

Miss Ziva was irritated. "Why don't you give them some advice?" Her eyes are as hard as metal screws. Once she wanted to rivet herself to the world with those eyes, but she didn't succeed. Once we went for a walk in the fields, her nylon stockings ripped on a thornbush, and she became angry with me. To this day she traverses the world with those hard blue eyes. Why had she come to me?

I was being called from the street. "Wait just a minute," I said, "one more mother." "I can't begin to tell you," said the mother when she came, "what a nuisance my naughty girl has been to me ever since she lay in my belly."

Bergman went off to an adjoining room to chat with the other teachers. The shadows under his eyes were like the shadows cast by a cloud that refuses to pass. His wife must say to him, "You have to get ahead in the world!" So he gets ahead, but the cloud beneath his eyes recalls him to the starting point. Bergman is a surveyor; what does he do? He goes out every morning and plants his black and white rods deep in the waste-land, gazing into the distance like a prophet: here will be houses, here will be gardens and cemeteries! I, on the other hand, have to prophesy about the men who will live in these houses. He always has his queer equipment about him. His poles, his theodolite, his scrolls, his registers, his calculations.

Bergman unbuttoned his overcoat to show me how his lapel was torn like a mourner's. Then he unbuttoned his shirt and took out his undershirt. I saw that even his chest bore the print of dried mud, just like the transports. "You see," he said to me, "I too." Men used to sprinkle ashes on their heads as a sign of mourning; now they cake themselves with earth because of the war. Bergman rearranged his clothing and left me with the globe, whose surface had peeled away with the years. A compass and a ruler hung from a hook: these delude the children no less than the teachers, because they foster the illusion that there is really such a thing as a straight line and a pure angle. The picture of the living President stared at the picture of the dead President. The picture of Bialik hung aslant and I straightened it. My favorite pupil entered the room. I patted her on the cheek, smudging her complexion with earth, like Bergman's chest and the cars. "What fun it will be," she said to me happily, "now I too can go to your war!"

When I left, it was already night and my wife was waiting for me at the bottom of the stairs. How did she know I was here? Her hair rustled and the briars rustled and there was a smell of burning in the air and her eyes grew black like after the Great Fire. "Come," I said to her, "we will go wake up some men so that the army may be brought up to full strength." The first person on our list was a milkman, whose hallway smelt of milk. We entered the courtyard; there are no longer many like it in Jerusalem. By the entrance there once lived an old professor from Czechoslovakia who came here with the escaping Czech army. How he came to be a professor and how he arrived here with the army, I don't know. He lived in a decrepit structure which had one wall adjacent to a ceramics kiln. He was always worrying that this house might go up in flames. He was feeble and emaciated like a dwarf, and though he dwelt above the ground, he lived, as dwarfs do, in the subterranean caverns of his soul. His voice was high and quavering like that of a mouse. Besides him, there lived in the old house an ancient bookbinder, whose sons were scattered about the world. While they drifted over the face of the earth as if swept by gusts of wind, he stuck to his post and fussily tended his books. His two youngest sons were arrested by the British police at the door of his bindery for illegal possession of weapons. The owner of the house was an Armenian doctor who lived in the Old City. Tall, thin and sharp-featured, he put in an appearance every now and then. There was also a storage bin for green vegetables, and sacks of peanuts and more vegetables were piled in a small courtyard.

One room was always rented to independent young girls, the kind who come to Jerusalem to study at the Music Conservatory or at the Bezalel Art School, and take up rug weaving or work in ceramics. They are always independent. When it suits their mood they have a gentleman caller, and when it suits their mood otherwise they kick him out through the courtyard. All day long they are always laundering something. On the top floor was a small school for little girls: the floorboards above the rooms creak with footsteps all day and sharp screams punctuate the recesses. Once I sat in one of those rooms and held an eight-day-old baby on my knees, held him forcibly because he was being circumcised. Afterwards there were little cakes and neighbors, and the wine flowed forlornly into the guests and into that sea which is the receptacle for everything.

My friend the soldier, whom I wished to remind of his military duty, sat by the potter's wheel. He was a potter and worked with clay. Behold the potter in the hands of his clay, I thought to myself. I reversed all the proverbs I knew, and I saw that nothing ever changes in this world. You can bury the living and quicken the dead and nothing will change. "Wait a moment," said the soldier, "I want to finish this pitcher." The shelves along the wall were lined with scores of pitchers waiting to dry. Much time and much quiet ripening is needed for anything to be finished and perfect. In wartime, however, the unfinished is taken along with the finished, the dry with the wet. Boys are promoted to the rank of adults and ripen too quickly. Whoever breaks, breaks, and those who return no longer have the patience to sit and await their turn like those pitchers. They want to be useful and functional right away. They want a coat of glaze before they are even dry. Later, when the cracks begin to appear, they will be irreparable.

The potter took his rifle from underneath his bed and began to clean it: the barrel and the breechblock and the two sights, far and rear. I have seen many sights in my life. I told him where to go and departed. I waited at the bus stop with my wife. The bus came and she got on. The doors shut and she reached for her fare. She handed the driver a large bill and he had to stop his vehicle and give her change. All her life she has paid for everything with large bills. She sat by the window, resting her head against the back of the seat. The bus lurched forward and disappeared, and she shouted something at me from the window which I couldn't make out. Her speech is like a patch of cloud. When will the rain come? I was overcome by a terrible fear that soon I would be lying mangled and in need of patching on the field adjoining the hill.

I decided to go to the observation post to see the hill by night. I came to the house. A bicycle leaned against the door. Whose was it? The girl stood in the doorway and said, "I knew you would come."

"Perhaps you want your back wiped?"

"You have a dirty mind. Have you got a cigarette?"

"I don't smoke. What are you trying to do to me?"

"I'm not doing anything to you."

"Why are you wearing a red skirt?"

I tried to get past but she wouldn't let me: Don't look at your hill, look at me! I forced my way and she clung to me. I broke free and manacled her with the bicycle lock. "Don't go away," I said, "don't go, soon I'll be down again." I climbed the stairs to another apartment which was unoccupied and bored through the wall until I could see. The hill was bathed in moonlight. I saw shadowy men shoveling earth like gravediggers; the sound of metal striking against stone reverberated through the air. I added some lines and semicircles to my map, while on a separate slip of paper I wrote: assembly point, evacuation route, two machine guns, preliminary range finding, searchlights, ammunition crates in the small yard. I jotted down a few more notes in the same fashion. When I came downstairs the girl was still standing there, but the bicycle chain was broken. She doesn't know that all will be destroyed.

"Even though I broke loose, I waited for you." She stood like a heavy white cloud in the darkness.

"There isn't a chance in the world," I said to her.

"What are those clouds for?"

"The Nile is overflowing its banks."

"The Nile overflows its banks every year. Why don't you have any children? I'd come and be their nurse." She kept me company to the top of the street where we were stopped by a soldier hiding in a bread truck. I gave the password and we went on. Afterwards, I walked her home, and we stood on either side of the clothesline. Her black sleeveless dress had been hung up to dry. It was inside-out, and she stood beside it very sure of herself.

"How old are you?"

"Seventeen."

"Such a big girl, and your navel hasn't even healed yet."

"Silly boy, would you like to take a look?"

"Your navel has healed, but your eyes have not healed. After the separation your eyes will never heal. Once you were in the womb of the world. When you came forth and they cut your cord you were separated, and were no longer part of it. That's why you long for it, and your eyes have not healed." She laughed and fended me off with her hand: "Go on, go on, you and your maps and your plans." "It's because the plans are as sad as my face," I said to her. "Your face, my dear, has no sadness and no plans and is unprepared for the future."

A sergeant passed by. "Walk along with me," he said, "I have to get my army boots." His army boots were in storage where his old father and mother live. He himself is married and has children and a home of his own, but he leaves his army boots with his parents. His old mother brought him a ladder. He went up to the attic and disappeared there to search. His mother looked at me. "Why are they calling you?" she asked. I shrugged my shoulders.

That night signs of the impending battle multiplied in the blacked-out city. Cars drove through the streets at a whisper, children ceased to shout. My wife took in the wash from the roof; women soldiers dressed in pajamas stood by the antennas and spoke into space. Work tools were readied in the cemeteries, and secret arsenals were opened in grocery stores and beneath monuments and sleeping men. Outdoors, human chains passed crates from hand to hand in the square. Jews maddened by the Psalms stood in courtyards, trumpeters and drummers practiced in the youth centers. Proclamations were pasted to human backs. Rams' horns were tested, and new machinery and freshly lubricated hopes were brought out into the open. Arms were cached underground. Hearts were tested. Soldiers rested beneath their blankets in driveways, like candleless dead. Queues formed before the cinemas, men picked each other clean of memories, like old notices stripped from a bulletin board, in order to be ready and not weighed down by past events. At the entrance to the city, each citizen received the Insignia of the Holy Earth. Man and his engines preserve Thou, O Lord! Ambulances drove by masked with flapping nets, like the veils on the Bride of Death. Women blessed the Sabbath candles though it was only a weekday. Girls in hoop skirts parachuted in the public squares. Metallic sounds filled the air. Commands were whispered. Loudspeakers were set up. Silent speakers frightened the sleepers.

The following day kindergarten children were driven to the border and told to dance and play for the sake of camouflage. Young girls were brought and told to wear colorful clothing with bright buttons for the sake of camouflage. In the evening pairs of lovers were transported and told to make love before the enemy's eyes for the sake of camouflage, so that the enemy might not see the preparations for the terrible battle.

My captain came and said, "We have to find another house from which we can see the southern side of the hill." We circled the hill like Balaam and Balak. "Just a minute," I said, "just a minute." My wife's hand was firmly in my own. Big hands must hold little hands: this is their duty in the world. My wife looked at my captain with hostility. "I too have left my wife and children," he said. My captain showed us pictures of his wife and children. They smiled the way people smile on the pictures you find in the pockets of dead soldiers. We approached the sentry, who was our grocer, but was now guarding the way. "Your wife can go no further," he said; "from here on the front begins." He gave her a jar of yogurt, some plum jelly and a few other provisions, and she went home. She was too weighed down to turn around, but I watched her go. It was well that she had her hands full with the jars she was carrying. From here on I was deeply engrossed in conversation with my captain.

"They've added four new positions during the night."

"And they've added rolls of barbed wire there, a whole sea of barbed wire, and mines near the red house in the southern valley."

"This will be our assembly point. It has water, drainage and sewerage. It has an exit and an entrance to the world."

"Where will we set up the machine guns?"

"Many will fall."

A Yemenite boy came along and we bought two sticks of ice cream from him. We sucked them until only the sticks were left. We took the sticks and traced out a map on the ground, pointing with them as one does with the pointer of a Torah scroll. More officers joined the conference. They all scratched lines and dots in the ground, manipulating little stones and bigger stones. I pretended I was going to urinate and left the circle. As soon as I gained the nearest corner I began to run, stopping only when I had reached home. My wife was not there, so I stood by the window. Now that I was preparing to leave again, I noticed for the first time the trees in the garden beyond the wall. A breeze stirred them, and they swayed as if in the act of love.

Our wall touched the next wall. The next wall nudged the next house with its shoulder, as if to pass on the news. Were I King Solomon, I would know what they were saying about the coming battle. I lowered my head. My head was like a flag at half-mast. Only then did I spy the slip of paper, left for me by my wife on the coffee table:

"I'm at mother's, come."

I marveled that the slip should be faded and yellow like a Dead Sea Scroll, for the note had been written only today and the paper had been white and fresh. Under the kites flown by the children, I skirted the city. In a nook where I had once made love, by the very rock, a sentry sat cooking himself a meal. He pointed at the kites in the sky and at the charred trunks of the olive trees. He pointed because his mouth was busy chewing. At his side lay a compass in which a needle nervously revolved. A boy ran after a dog which he held on a leash. What were they chasing, who chased them? A cannon stood in readiness beneath a lattice-work of thorns. I approached my mother's house from the valley, so that she had no advance warning. The road was inscribed with chalk arrows, all pointing in the same direction, as in a children's game. I practically followed them all the way. The quarter in which my mother lives is a small one, and is inhabited by artists and students and lofty trees and Yemenites and Germans and old settlers of Jerusalem who work in the foundations and the labor federation. Often when I am leaving the area on Saturday nights, I see crowds of people climbing the steps which lead into it. A young couple, pressed against each other; two girls, one pretty and the other with musclebound legs, returning from their youth center. The neighborhood swallows them all. A young man pushes a perambulator up the steps

and his wife carries the baby. Dogs and cats. Even the
letter-carrier who brings the mail. I have seen him only
entering the neighborhood, never leaving it—as if it
refused to let him go. The same for the milkman, and
another pair of lovers, who stroll side by side touching
palms. Somebody is always playing the piano in my
mother's neighborhood. Sometimes the late sonatas of
Beethoven, sometimes the early sonatas of first love.
The neighborhood swallows them all, and is never too
full and never short of space. They never build new
houses in it, or add new stories to the old ones. Many
of the apartments can be reached only by means of
winding, open-air staircases. There is even a small public park, planted in honor of a soldier, a neighborhood
boy, who was killed. His father comes daily to water
the trees. He leans over to water them with love, and
the trees grow straight and their leaves are shiny.
Sometimes the girl who plays the piano places a sprig
of glossy eucalyptus leaves where her heart is. When her
boy friend comes home from the army he kneads the
leaves, and the pungent smell reaches his nose. The
neighborhood slopes toward the valley. Women set out
their laundry and boys send up their kites, and all find
their way to heaven.

I asked my mother for some sacks which might be
filled with sand and used for protection against bombardment. My mother's attic is spacious, and full of old
costumes for Purim masquerades. She took the pouch
which held my father's prayer shawl, filled it with sand
and sewed old clothes together into additional sacks—
all because it was an emergency. I ate standing up. My
wife was not there and came only at the last minute.
She went with me to the assembly point. I noticed that
the garden wall was caving in, that the well was empty
and that the trenches by the roadside gaped as widely

as ever. We walked through the narrow alleyways; it was afternoon and the streets were clear. A soldier stood on top of a high building, signaling with flags to a distant place. I signaled to myself inwardly, to my blood, which was sufficiently alarmed as it was. My sister stood in a telephone booth, placing a call. She could not let go of the receiver, but she gesticulated at me with her head. While her mouth talked into the distance, her eyes conversed with me. We have always had good times together, and now perhaps I am going to meet my death. When we were children we divided the world between us. Even when we were angry with each other and came to blows, we fought wisely and with a plan; I would turn my back to her and let her beat me with clenched fists without resisting. Then it would be my turn to beat her, and she would sit and not interfere. With that, the quarrel was over. Though we disagreed, we never enjoyed the blows, and our ears were insensitive to that wonderfully resonant drum, the pummeled body.

We reached the designated corner. My captain was waiting with some other members of the company. The truck was due in three minutes. My captain was angry because I had run away. He removed his eyeglasses, so as not to see the tears in the eyes of the women. I deposited the bag of candies on the ground; the paper was beginning to rip, and the colored wrappers sparkled. The truck arrived, covered with drying mud. The motor started. "It begins tonight," whispered my captain into my ear. I knew that I would never see my wife again. It was a winter day, but her face was as dry as if it had been parched by a sirocco. She didn't want to cry but the tears came. Her whole body shared them, her hands and her legs, her hair and her thighs, until her torso became heavy and only her face remained dry. When we began to move it was like an eclipse of the moon. The side of the house encroached upon her fine, round face. Slowly the wall surged forward, until her face was completely covered. As she walked home she rocked back and forth a little. Her blood cried like an infant. She had to calm it. Her body was like a cradle for her blood, but the more she rocked it the harder it cried.

The truck jolted on and we rocked in it like drunkards. "It's apparently scheduled for tonight," said my captain, "but I'm not entirely sure. We'll have to billet the company." We found a house still in the process of construction. Part of it lay buried beneath wooden planks; the ceiling was dripping, for the concrete had only been poured the day before and a series of posts held it in place. We started to change our clothing: short pants for long, and long for short. The men scattered through the building. The rooms, which were not quite finished, rang with their voices. The practical jokers went about saying: This is the bathroom. This is the tub. I'm a gorgeous lady, soaping herself naked.

We sat upon sacks of cement near some barrels of whitewash, watching the patchy sky through blank windows. The night passed in a steady medley of men alighting from trucks and the clomp of boots, doors slamming and heavy utensils falling angrily. We lay in a small, empty room. The runner lay down at our feet. By his side were the machine gun, the ram's horn, and the evening paper. We were awakened frequently during the night by the arrival of reinforcements; shadowy men stood outside like beggars, waiting for us to find them a place and distribute arms. My captain got up in the middle of the night and left. When he returned, he proceeded to shine his flashlight on the sleeping men. He held a fresh packet of papers in his hand, like a bouquet—collections of orders. We got up and took our bearings anew; the enemy had strengthened the hill. There were cannon and minefields and women crying in village doorways. Some of the mines were exploding already, through mental telepathy. We were forced to revise the entire assault.

We crisscrossed the city, distributing ammunition. Everybody received a package. We hid ammunition in milk buckets, in toy boxes and underneath our hats, so that the enemy would not know where it was. In the morning, when we went to observe the hilltop, we saw that a change had come over it—like a body covered with freckles, it was arrayed with redoubts and fresh trenches. There were no shadows, and the wind piled the clouds in a high bank. I went to school. I meant to place a book upon the table, but instead I put down some bullets and an empty canteen. The children were wild and refused to settle down. The young teacher erased the board with her long hair and smiled at me. She was my substitute. I drew a plan of the hill on the blackboard with different colored chalk. "This is new territory," I said. "We will learn all about it." I drew arrows, dotted lines, circles and crosses. The teacher laid her hand on my shoulder and said in a sad voice, "Calm down, relax!" I erased the board and left. I ran all the way home; it was already evening, it was night. My wife was asleep; I didn't wake her. The world was quiet, and I lay on my back. The light from the neighbors' window cast an illuminated square upon the ceiling. People drifted home from their reveling. The young couple whose wedding picture I had seen somewhere in a photographer's box returned home too. The bride's voice was husky, sweet and honeyed in its lower register. Perhaps she sings too much at parties. Doors closed—of houses, of motorcars, of people. My eyes were wide open. Trucks passed, going in different directions. This reassured me. Had they been going in the same direction it would mean that the battle was starting; since they went in different directions, they meant no harm. I debated whether to wake my wife or let her sleep. Opportunities to talk are few. Always the stillness before the noise, and always the noise before the stillness. In the noise we cannot hear one another. In the stillness we cannot talk for fear of being overheard. I lay on my stomach, taking cover behind the pillow. In my mind's eye I saw the terrible hill. That very moment the area under barbed wire was being enlarged. An ocean of barbed wire. Half the company would be mowed down. I was about to doze off when there came a knock on the door. The front bell rang. The company clerk was pale: "Come at once!" I dressed silently. The clerk had already gone ahead; he descended many steps, some of which weren't even there. My wife sat on the bed, hugging her knees close to her body, as if to say: these have remained loyal and stayed with me. I snatched a sweater from the chest of drawers. All the sweaters tumbled out, red ones and yellow ones, hers and mine. My wife sobbed like a child who has been roused from its sleep. I am going out to die. This time I said my good-bys to her forehead, rather than to her mouth or hand. Behind the hard forehead soft thoughts dwell, and beyond where thoughts harden, soft hair.

I went downstairs. I wanted to do it quietly, but my spiked boots shattered the silence. I headed for the unfinished building. Along the narrow walled pavement, a former pupil of mine knelt to fix her shoes. I asked her why she sat there after midnight. She looked me up and down, while her hands attended to the shoes.

"How was it on the kibbutz? Didn't you go to a kibbutz after finishing your studies?"

"It was lovely, but I've been left all alone. They've all gone off to the war, and my shoes have torn."

I saw that she had grown up and would no longer listen to me. My pupils are scattered all over the world. One is already dead. I had no time to talk with the girl. She looked pretty in the beam of the flashlight. She squatted on one heel, fixing the shoe on the opposite foot. As she sat, her body seemed to fill out. Not so my thoughts, which were pointed like the prow of a ship. Why had she run away from home? I'm not going to war. The war is by my front step. The gate to my house is the beginning of the front. "I don't understand you," she said. "When I was your pupil I never understood you either; then you used to scold me. Now I'm grown up and pretty, and I sit before you in the night between two walls and my thighs are full."

A motorcyclist drove up, blinding me with his lights; he drew to a stop, and I hopped onto the back seat. The girl continued to squat on the pavement. Perhaps she saw an angel, blocking the road with drawn sword, someone I could not see. I came to the building; no one was there but the old watchman. The barrels of white-wash were where I had left them, as was the dripping from the concrete roof. A cat crossed between the watchman and me. "They left an hour ago," he said. "See, the papers are still fluttering on the spot where company headquarters was. Here is a strap that was left behind." I picked up a buckle from some piece of equipment. Where is my buckle, where does my life fasten? The buckle is death. It fits practically any strap. I threw the buckle away and wandered through the city, searching for my company. An engineering unit was throwing a temporary iron bridge across the square. I asked why they were building it but received no an-swer. A lone cannon rolled silently down the street on rubber wheels, until it ran into a telephone pole and came to a halt. An overturned car lay at the intersection, its wheels still spinning in the air. A pair of lovers came by and crawled into the cabin, sitting there upside-down while the wheels turned above them. I remembered a soldier in my unit who lived in an abandoned British army base. In order to get there I had to cut across an alleyway. "So you've forgiven me, have you?" cried a voice from the cellar. Bending over, I caught sight of Nissim; myopic Nissim with the thick lenses, who was forever breaking his glasses and having to get a new pair made. He had never learned to fire a rifle, and we hadn't bothered to call him. He left the cellar, however, tagging along behind me until we reached the deserted base. Nothing was left of it but a couple of old stoves, a few ramshackle bungalows and an outhouse. Many things were scrawled on the walls of the outhouse: "Out of bounds!" "Officers only!" "For children!" "Auxiliary corps for women only!" Over these was written in Hebrew: "Men." "Ladies." "Company D." "Yoska is an ass." "Down with German rearmament!" "General John, go home!" "For shame!" "On with Spanish rearmament!"

I stood beneath the sign which said "Out of bounds," but I was definitely within bounds. Bounded by death and by destiny. I saw the soldier I had been looking for sitting amongst some ruins, reading a book. His beard was short and fluffy, and he had a face like Jesus. When I seized him he said, "I still haven't caught up on my sleep from the last mobilization. I need a great deal of sleep to nourish my thoughts." I sent Nissim to have his glasses repaired because they broke. I was left with the soldier who resembled Jesus. The wire fence was like the crown of thorns placed around his head. A truck came by and we were handed a spool of telephone wires. The two of us grabbed a pole, and passing it through the cylinder we began to walk. There were many kinds of wire, in several colors. Wires for good news and for bad news, and wires for whispered longings, such as: Where are you?

I'm forbidden to say.
Raise your voice.
It's forbidden to raise it.
Raise your head.
It's raised.
I wish I could see you.
I'm like the receiver in your hands: ears to speak with and a mouth to listen.

We walked and walked until the wire ran out. We put down the empty metal spool. Children came and played with it, rolling it about. Girls jumped rope with the colored wires. We passed on, treading on the chalk lines drawn by the children. The game the children play is not to step on the lines, but to jump over them. We stepped on them. God, or somebody like Him, does the same to us—as soon as we draw up rules and lines and boundaries, He comes with his monstrous feet and steps on them, because He doesn't care.

We came to a courtyard by the edge of the city which had an observation post. Every point in Jerusalem is a beachhead but everything is dry and there is no ocean of water. Yet the sea of Jerusalem is the most terrible sea of all. Every place in Jerusalem is a tongue of the city—and the city has many tongues and nobody understands her. I have tried many times to cut my ties with Jerusalem, and each time I have remained. If I come back safe and sound from the battle on the hill, I shall never return to Jerusalem!

I walked on, and as I walked I thought, a thinking

man walking along a street always looks beaten. A man walking in a khaki uniform is better off not thinking. One day they will arrest him and call him a traitor and demand to know his thoughts. My thoughts finally brought me to a narrow valley; my company was camped beneath the olive trees. I had not even had time to sit down before I was besieged with requests for passes. I had to give every man an answer, and no man was dispensable.

He said, "I'm a storekeeper, the margarine is streaming though the cracks in the door."

I answered, "My longings for my wife are also streaming."

He said, "I haven't received my pay yet."

I answered, "Your children will collect your pay for you."

He said, "They won't give it to them without my signature."

I answered, "I have my signature and I still don't know who I am."

He said, "It's the anniversary of my father's death, I want to recite the mourner's prayer."

I answered, "We are all dying, and the clouds will rain upon us, and there's no need to pray."

Hours passed, and I grew weary. Doctors and nurses came to examine our blood; a nurse jabbed her needle into a stray vein. A doctor saw the blood and said, "It's no good."

All the officers who were to take part in the attack gathered together. Artillery experts came to coordinate the shelling, chaplains to coordinate the aid of Providence, and every now and then somebody brought his wife. "It's good for the women to see that it's not so terrible," said our captain. Once more we attacked the hill and made calculations. Man and his guns preserve

Thou, O Lord! Information arrived which put an entirely different slant on things: what we had thought to be barbed wire was really men, and what we had thought to be bunkers were gun emplacements. Once more nothing was certain. Death alone was certain for all. I revised the map according to the latest information. My ink ran out. I borrowed a pen from my wife. The pen fell between the ammunition crates, on which was written: "Fragile, Handle with Care," "No Smoking, Explosive Material," "Keep In a Cool Dark Place." I too wanted to lie down in a cool dark place, and write "Handle With Care" on myself. I never found the pen, but the panic I experienced on the first night failed to return. Sometimes a great clarity strikes me flush between the eyes. Autumn days come, cleansing the troubled winds of summer. A group of soldiers crouched by a dip in the valley and played at Questions and Answers. I knew that on the following evening they would be asking no questions, but would be lying in wait for the zero hour. Among a patrol of riflemen I met my little pupil Mazal, who is seven years old. She has large eyes, her mother is a slut and her father is an Arak drinker. "I'm going off to the war with you," she said. "I'm a nurse, and I have a white cap and a white apron left over from Purim."

"You have to go home. Your mother will worry."

"She won't worry."

"And your little brothers?"

"I've already taken care of them and fixed them some food."

"It's not Purim now. You have to go to school."

"They don't let me go because I have lice in my hair. The teacher made me leave."

"Rinse your hair with kerosene and have it cut!"

She shook her black curls. "I won't cut it, I'm going to war with you. If I cut it I won't be strong. Didn't we learn about Samson?"

"But a little girl like you has to keep clean," I told her.

She threw me a long look which traveled from one end of Jerusalem to the other. I sat her down in the playground which had been converted into the evacuation center for the wounded. She started to play with the dolls. She listened to their heartbeat and gave them injections. One of the dolls was exuding dry seaweed and she bandaged it. Chairs scraped overhead; I could tell that the staff meeting was over. I heard men jumping into trucks, the clank of metal, and meters turning over. My captain came in and saw Mazal, but said nothing; he waved the bundle of papers in his hand. I grabbed hold of Mazal and we climbed together to the attic. We could see the hill. "Your eyes are tired," she said, "let me look." I gave her the binoculars.

"What do you see, Mazal?"

"Men standing and passing green crates."

"What else?"

"Many sacks, and barbed wire like a lot of curls."

"What else?"

"Now they're hiding. All I see is bushes and mounds of dirt."

I came down with Mazal from the observation post and asked my wife to take her home. They linked hands and disappeared. Everything is always disappearing, and I can retain nothing. "Where is the young girl?" I asked the tenants, "the one who sings in the bathtub?" She had gone to a party for the American marines who work at the Consulate. I stood in the doorway. Tracers lit the night, but the eternal light within my brain flickered silently and feebly. I went to the American building. A row of colored bottles stood against the wall. I watched the girl dance; her crinolines flapped about her waist, a red crinoline and a black one and a white one. She didn't notice me. She only stopped dancing when her thighs grew chilly. The American marines laughed, and she joined in their laughter. The American flag rippled like waves. I stepped outside. I passed a hard wall. I wanted to press myself against the terrible wall of history, like Rashi's mother.* I wanted to find myself a niche safe from an intransigent History. I wanted a miracle to come to pass, so I should not have to lie mutilated on the hillside.

I returned to my pup-tent. I thought a lot. I heard a voice saying, "At exactly eleven-fifty-eight we begin the bombardment." I thought some more. Finally, I raised my hand and switched off my thoughts the way you switch off a bed lamp. I was awakened frequently during the night. I imagined I was being called. I fell asleep again. A cold wind blew through the valley, slicing it open like a knife gutting fish. In the morning I couldn't tell whether there had been an attack or not. We continued to observe the hill. The earth was like those Christian saints who suffer from stigmata on their hands and feet, where the nails passed through Jesus and the cross. The earth was like them, bursting open where the shells were due to fall.

We strengthened our positions. We filled sandbags, and went off with our girl friends and wives to make love. We strolled down the streets, singing and dancing. One day a soldier approached me and I asked him what unit he belonged to. "I have no unit," he answered. "What is that insignia on your shoulder?" "It's not an insignia. It's a patch. My shirt ripped." I noticed

* According to an old Jewish legend, the mother of Rashi, the famous eleventh century Biblical exegete, was walking one day in a narrow, walled-in street in Worms during her pregnancy. A carriage came toward her and she was in danger of being crushed; she pressed herself against the wall behind, and the wall miraculously opened to receive her.

that some of his front teeth were missing. The company runner appeared, and I recalled that it was my job to see about hot drinks. I requisitioned a number of soldiers and we set off with empty buckets in our hands. We went to the large kitchen in the basement. It was not yet daybreak. Shouting to make themselves heard, the cooks moved among the lurid flames as if they were in Hell. "Where is the tea?" I shouted. The head cook pointed to a bucket. An oily, metallic, vaporous smell filled the air. We passed through the small courtyard, skidding on our boots. A fine rain began to fall. From the communications office came the laughter of the women operators. We put down our buckets and peered through the lighted windows. Even then the tea refused to calm down. All we saw in the window was the light.

That whole day the men practiced rapid mobilization. First they were told to go to work, and they went. Then the alarm was sounded, and they were made to lie in the trenches, in readiness for the attack. By evening we had reached a terrific speed of mobilization—the men threw away their work tools on the double and were handed rifles. In this manner I managed to spend part of my time in school. I appeared suddenly from behind a map of Asia Minor, frightening the children. My captain came in the night: Now it's in earnest! I looked him in the eyes.

"You're joking."

"No, this time it's serious."

The men were already asleep in their jumping-off positions. We went to take a last look. The streets were empty, and the vacant lots were hoarse as if from too much shouting. We lay down in a briar patch opposite the hill. My captain and I dozed off from time to time. In the early hours of the morning I suddenly asked,

"How much longer?" He shook his head, and the bushes rustled by his shoulder. At daybreak I noticed that the bush above my head was larger than my head, and larger than the rising sun. I noticed that the dry grass beside me swayed and trembled, while the grass in the distance was tranquil. The world resembles men who are all looking around a corner at the same thing. I watch them from a distance, and cannot tell what it is they find so fascinating. We went to sit at a marble table in a small restaurant and made a complete inventory: the delivery of weapons after the hill was taken and the evacuation of the wounded. We heard the clanking of metal. My captain jumped to his feet and shouted, "The tanks are coming!" We saw there were no tanks, only a truck piled high with bottles. We laughed. Rather than look at the enemy hill, I looked towards the city. I saw men walking about and children playing, and I could not go back. Towards evening my men began to abandon their positions one by one, slipping away to their homes. I tried to stop them. "Let them go," said my captain. "Soon they will come back anyway." I took my wife by the hand, and as we walked I told her about the hill. Every Saturday we go to look at it. Now and then I see my captain. Once, while sitting in the barber's chair to have my hair cut, I glanced in the mirror and saw my captain passing in the street. Sometimes my whole life passes before my eyes in the barber's mirror. I jumped from the chair. I paid for my haircut, and rushed out to the street to run after him. My captain was already gone.

—Translated by Hillel Halkin

S. Y. AGNON

Forevermore

*"Forevermore" is among the
most beautifully written—
and the most elusive—of
Agnon's allegories. Various
symbolic interpretations have
been suggested for the letters
A and G (Hebrew* ayin *and*
gimal*), which recur as initials throughout the story.
Among other things, they
are, of course, the first two
letters of the author's name.*

For twenty years Adiel Amzeh worked on his history of the great city of Gumlidata, the pride of mighty nations until it was reduced to dust and ashes by the Gothic hordes, and its people enslaved.

After he had gathered all his researches together, examined and tested them, sorted, edited, and arranged them, he decided that his work was finally ready for publication and he sat down and wrote the book he had planned for so many years. He took the book and made the rounds of the publishers but without success. He looked about for patrons and benefactors but had no luck. During all the years he had been occupied with his research he had not taken the trouble to ingratiate himself with the learned men of the universities—nor with their wives and daughters—and now when he came to them seeking a favor, their eyes shone with such cold anger that their glasses seemed to warp. "Who are you, sir?" they said to him. "We've never seen you before." Amzeh shrugged his shoulders and went away disappointed and dejected. He understood that in order to be recognized he would have to become friendly with them and he had no idea of how to go about it. Many years of painstaking research had made him a slave to his work from dawn till night, neglectful of all worldly cares. When he left his bed in the morning, his feet would carry him to the desk, his hands would pick up pen and paper, and his eyes, if not pursuing some obscure vision, would plunge into a book or into maps and sketches of the city and its great battles; and when he lay down to sleep he would go over his notebooks again, sometimes consciously, sometimes hardly realizing what he was doing. Years passed and his book remained unpublished. You know, a scholar who is unable to publish his work often benefits from the delay, since he can re-examine his assumptions and correct his errors, testing those hypotheses that may seem far from historical reality and truth.

Finally, when he had despaired of ever seeing the results of his work in print, his luck took a turn for the better. Gebhard Goldenthal, the richest man in the city, informed him that he would publish the book. How did it happen that the name of a humble scholar had reached the ear of this famous rich man? And why would such an eminent personage want to publish a work which was sure to bring no profit? Some said he felt so uneasy about his great wealth that he had decided to become a patron of learning in order to salve his conscience. He followed closely the world of scholarship and somehow had heard the story of Adiel Amzeh's book. According to another explanation, Gebhard Goldenthal secretly believed that his ancestors were among the unhappy people who were driven out of Gumlidata, that they had belonged to the city's aristocracy and that one of them had been an army general, the head of the palace guard. Of course, this was obviously untrue since Gumlidata was destroyed during the first wave of the Gothic invasions when the whole civilized world was turned upside down. No person can say with any certainty that he is a descendant of the exiles of Gumlidata. But whatever the reason, Gebhard Goldenthal was ready to publish Adiel Amzeh's book, even though printing this kind of work would involve many extra expenses. Several colored maps were necessary, requiring many expensive inks: one for a general view of the city, another for its temples, a third for each of its gods—Gomesh, Gush, Gutz, Guach, and Guz; one for the founding mothers of the city, one for its apostates, another for Gomed the Great, one for Gichur and Amul—the twin pillars of prayer—and one each for all the remaining holy men, the priests and priestesses, not to mention the temple prostitutes and the dogs and all the saints—for each and every one a different color, to denote position and function. Add to all these the Goths and their allies, their carts and wagons, their weapons and battle defenses, and you can see how much money was needed to print such a work. Nevertheless, Gebhard Goldenthal was ready to publish the book and make it a fine volume with beautiful printing and good paper, carefully detailed maps, expensive binding—perfect in every respect. His staff had already consulted with illustrators, engravers, and printers, and all that remained was for the author and publisher to meet, for in all his business affairs Gebhard Goldenthal would allow his staff to take care of the preliminaries, but the final arrangements had to be conducted between the client and the head of the business himself. If the client was unknown, he would be invited to Goldenthal's office; if the man was recognized in his field, he might be invited for a cup of tea to Goldenthal's home; and if he was important, he would be invited for dinner. Adiel Amzeh, who was more than a nobody but not well-known enough to be considered important, was invited by the rich man for a cup of tea.

So it was that one day Adiel Amzeh received an invitation for afternoon tea at the home of Gebhard Goldenthal. He was asked to be prompt and come at the designated hour since Mr. Goldenthal was soon leaving for abroad and was pressed for time.

An author who for years has searched without avail for a publisher is not likely to be late for an appointment with the one he has finally found. Almost before he put down his publisher's invitation, he took out his best suit of clothes—untouched since the day he received his doctor's degree—shook it out and pressed it. He hurried to the barber, and from the barber to the bath; from there he ran to a shop where he bought a new tie, and from the shop back home to look over his book again. By morning of the day of his appointment, he had made all his preparations for his visit to the publisher. Never in his life had he experienced such a day as this. Adiel Amzeh, who for the sake of a city's destruction had put aside all personal affairs, who cared nothing for clothes or any human vanity, was utterly changed. He had become like most celebrated learned men who neglect their work for the sake of the honor they receive from others who know nothing of learning and scholarship. He sat and stared at his manuscript, rose and inspected himself in the mirror, glanced at his watch, examined his clothes, and rehearsed his gestures. This is the regimen of all who wish to meet with a rich man. You must preen yourself and be careful of your demeanor and graces: the rich, even those who honor learning, prefer to honor it when it comes wrapped in a pleasing mantle. Yet that same love of learning which had used up so much of his energy and strength, furrowing his brow and bowing his shoulders, had touched his face with a special kind of radiance that one doesn't find except among those who are truly devoted to seeking wisdom. It's a pity Goldenthal never actually set eyes upon him; had he done so he might have realized that a pleasant and happy face can be shaped from things other than money. But you see, my friend, for the sake of a little moralizing, I have gone and given away the ending at the very beginning of my story.

Well, Amzeh sat for a while, then got up, sat down again, rose again—all the time thinking of the future when the printer would take up his manuscript and transform it into attractive pages; he thought of how he would correct proofs, add and delete, omit and include certain passages; of how the printer does his work and how his book would finally be published and received. Sitting there dreaming he might have missed the appointed hour, except that all the years he had devoted to his work had sharpened him in his external affairs as well. When the moment came for him to leave for his appointment, he jumped up from his chair, picked up his house key, and made ready to leave and lock the door behind him. He stared at himself in the mirror once more and glanced about his home, astonished that his house had not changed as he had. There ought to have been some transformation, he thought, for this would have been only just for a man who was about to undergo a blessed metamorphosis.

At that moment, he heard the sound of footsteps and suddenly became alarmed. Perhaps Mr. Goldenthal had to leave before the appointed time and someone was coming to tell him the interview had been postponed. Amzeh stood transfixed and could hardly catch his breath; his reason was gone, only his senses functioned. His entire body seemed to become one big ear. As he listened intently to the footsteps, he realized that he was hearing the slow shuffling of an old woman. In a moment, his powers of reason returned and he understood that a gentleman like Goldenthal would not send an old woman to deliver a note canceling their appointment. When the sound of the old woman's footsteps came closer, he recognized them as those of a nurse who visited him once each year in order to collect journals and illustrated magazines to take to the inmates of the lepers' hospital where she worked. It was difficult for Amzeh to put the old woman off by telling her he was busy and asking that she come the following year; he had high regard for this nurse who devoted her entire life to those whose existence was a living death. But it was equally hard for him to tarry on her account, for if he was delayed, with Mr. Goldenthal about to go abroad and no one knowing when he would return, then the publication of his book would also be postponed. I should mention another factor as well, which might seem unimportant but perhaps was decisive. To a man whose home is his whole universe, every unnecessary article in the house can cause annoyance. So it was with our scholar. When his mind was occupied with Gumlidata and he strolled through its ruins carrying on long conversations with the priests and holy men of the temple, he would occasionally raise his eyes and notice a pile of dusty old magazines. Now that the old woman had come, here was an opportunity to get rid of them; if he didn't act now, they would accumulate and gather dust for another year.

At the very moment when he was deciding what to do, whether to get rid of the superfluous volumes or to devote all his efforts to his own book, the old woman knocked on the door. He opened it and greeted her. The old woman understood immediately that he was worried and preoccupied, like a man uncertain whether to take an affirmative or negative course. "I see, Herr Doctor," she said, "that I have come at an inconvenient time. I'll leave and go about my business."

He was silent for a moment and didn't answer her. When she finally turned to go, he realized how tired the old woman must be from her long walk. After all, the lepers' home was far from the city, and she had to come on foot. She was unable to travel by autobus for fear that if recognized she would be thrown off—most people are still terrified by the sight of someone who works with lepers.

"I'm sorry," Amzeh said to her as she was about to go, "but I can't take care of you the way I would like. I have been invited to afternoon tea by Gebhard Goldenthal, the famous industrialist whose name you have probably heard." (As a matter of fact, forty years previously Gebhard Goldenthal had courted the nurse and wanted to marry her, but she refused him because she had already given her heart to God's maimed, the poor prisoners of the lepers' home.) "I have a very important matter to discuss with Mr. Goldenthal," Adiel Amzeh went on. "I'll be back in an hour or so. Please sit down until I return, and later I'll fill your basket with books and journals and pamphlets and anything else I have about—they take up so much room here I can hardly breathe."

"I would like to sit here and wait for you, Herr Doctor," the old woman answered, "but I can't leave my good people for more than a short while. They are used to me and I am used to them, and when I'm away from them I miss them as much as they miss me. They are used to receiving all their needs from me. I'll go now, Herr Doctor, and if God grants me life and peace, I'll come back next year."

But Amzeh was unable to let her go away like that, without an explanation of why he was in such a hurry. Without thinking about how little time he had, he began to explain: "Perhaps you have noticed my appearance today. For many years you have been coming to visit me and you have always found me with slippers on my feet and a cap on my head, unshaven, my collar open, my hair disheveled. Today I'm dressed in a good suit and wearing shoes and a hat and a nice tie. The reason for the change is simple: for twenty years I have worked on a book and it is finally ready for publication. Mr. Gebhard Goldenthal has decided to publish it, and I'm now going to see him. He's waiting for me and for my book."

A flush came over the old woman's face. "You mustn't delay a moment, Herr Doctor, hurry, hurry, don't wait, an hour like this doesn't come every day, don't put off even a minute what you have waited for for many years. It is good that you found Mr. Goldenthal. He's an honest man. He keeps his promises. But I'm not a very good friend, intruding on you at a time like this. I remember when I began to serve in the lepers' hospital, the rooms were full of dust and broken beds and chairs, the roof was caved in, the walls tottering and moldy. If he hadn't given us money to put the place together again, to buy new beds and equipment and make all the necessary repairs, it would have been impossible to get along there."

After the old woman had recounted all of Gebhard Goldenthal's good deeds, she let out a deep sigh. "Are you unhappy?" Adiel Amzeh asked her. "Unhappy?" she replied with a shy smile. "I've never been unhappy." He was quiet for a moment. "You are unique, Nurse Eden, you are the only one in the world who can make such a declaration," he said.

The old woman blushed with confusion. "I really should correct what I just said, Herr Doctor. I have had great unhappiness, but not of my own making." Her face turned scarlet and she lapsed into silence.

"You stopped right in the middle of what you were saying, Nurse Adeh," Amzeh said, "and perhaps at the crucial point. I'm certain it would be worthwhile to hear."

"Worthwhile?" the old woman cried, stammering in her effort to speak quickly. "How do we know what is worthwhile and what isn't? I'm an old woman whose grave is waiting for her—let me boast once that I told the whole truth. I flattered myself falsely when I said that I've never been unhappy. On the contrary, I haven't known a day without sorrow, a sorrow greater than that of my good people who suffer more than any other creatures in the world. For the merciful God who inflicts suffering on man provides him with the strength to withstand his woes; but if one is healthy and without physical disability, then he has no special allotment of strength, and when he looks on those who suffer and on their pain he is chastened and has nothing with which to withstand his sorrow. And especially someone like myself, who has to look after the suffering ones. I'm always afraid that I won't fulfill my obligations, that I don't devote enough of my time to the good people. Even if I leave them for a moment, their suffering does not leave me. . . . But I'm talking too much. I've forgotten that you are in a hurry. Now I'll be going. I hope, Herr Doctor, that your business will bring you a full life and peace. Only pity the poor people who must see me return empty-handed, without any books."

"Why pity them?" he asked, facing her. "Have they finished all the books? They've read them all?"

"They've read them hundreds of times," answered the old woman.

"What kind of books do they have?"

"Oh, I can give you the names of all of them."

"All of them? Surely you're exaggerating."

"No, there aren't very many. I've been there so many years, every article and every book is familiar to me."

The old woman then recited the name of each book in the hospital library. "Not many, not very many at all," Amzeh said after she had finished. "I can imagine how happy they must be to receive a new book. But," he went on, jokingly, "I'm sure you have forgotten one or two, and perhaps they were the best books of the lot. For that's the way we are—we always forget the most important thing. Isn't that so, Nurse Adeh?"

The old woman smiled. "I have no love of dialectics. But I must say for truth's sake that there isn't a book in our library that I haven't mentioned—except for one, which is hardly worth discussing, since it isn't read any more."

"Why isn't it read any more?"

"Why? Because it has decayed with age, and on account of the tears."

"On account of the tears?"

"Because of the tears, yes, because of the tears that every reader of the book shed on its pages after reading the awful tales it contains."

"What are these terrible stories?"

"I don't know what they are," the old woman answered. "Whatever I know I've told you already. It's an old, worn-out book, written on parchment. They say it was written more than a thousand years ago. Had I known you would ask, I would have made inquiries. There are still old men in the hospital who can tell the story, which I remember many years ago the old men before them used to tell with tears—the same story that is in the book. But they say that even then, years ago, the old men already had difficulty in reading the book because its pages were torn and the words blurred. The manuscript is a heap of moldy, decayed matter. There have been many requests to burn it. In my time one of the caretakers was all set to destroy it, but I asked him to return it. I told him that a book which had found shelter with us mustn't be treated like a dog. I believe, Herr Doctor, that a piece of work done by an artist gives joy to the creator as long as it endures."

"Tell me, Nurse Adeh," Amzeh said, mulling over the old woman's words, "perhaps you have heard something about the contents of the book. What do your old men say about it? I'm sure if they say anything at all, they must know more."

"I've heard that all its pages are of parchment," the old woman answered. "As far as what is written in it, I've heard that it contains the history of a city which was destroyed and disappeared from the face of the earth."

"A city which had been destroyed and disappeared from the world!" Amzeh repeated excitedly. "Please tell me, Nurse Eden, perhaps you have heard the name of the city?"

"Yes, I have heard the name. The name of the city is Gumlidata, yes, Gumlidata is the name."

"What? What? What?" Amzeh stammered, his tongue caught in his mouth. "Have . . . have . . . you heard the name correctly . . . ? Gum . . . Gum . . . Gumli . . . lidata . . . you said. Please, my good nurse, tell me again, what is the name of the city you mentioned? Guml. . . ."

She repeated what she had said. "Gumlidata is the name of the city, and the book is an account of its history."

Adiel Amzeh grasped a table in front of him, leaning forward so that he would not collapse and fall. The old woman noticed his sudden paling and moved to help him. "What is the trouble, Herr Doctor," she said staring at him, "are you ill? Is it your heart?"

He straightened up and pulled himself together. "It's nothing, my good nurse," he began with a smile, "there's nothing wrong with me. On the contrary, you have given me new life. Let me tell you about it. For twenty years I have devoted myself to the history of this same city. There isn't a piece of paper which mentions the city's name that I haven't read. If I were king, I could build the city anew, just as it was before its destruction. If you want, I'll tell you about the historical trips I have taken. I have walked in the city's markets, strolled in its streets and alleys, seen its palaces and temples. Oh, my good nurse, what headaches I've suffered from the walks I've taken there. And I know how it was destroyed, who took part in the destruction, the name of each and every tribe that helped reduce it to ruins, how many were killed by the sword, how many died of starvation and thirst, and how many perished from the plague that followed the war. I know everything except one detail—from which side Gediton's brigades entered the city, whether from the side of the great bridge which was called the Bridge of Valor, or whether they entered secretly by way of the Valley of Aphardat, that is, the Valley of the Cranes . . . the plural of crane in the language of Gumlidata is *aphardat;* the word does not mean ravens or chestnut trees or overshoes as some linguists believe. In point of fact, 'raven' in the language of Gumlidata is *eldag* and in the plural *elgadata,* since when the letters 'd' and 'g' come together in the plural they reverse their order. I don't know the words for chestnut trees or overshoes in the language of Gumlidata. I really don't know what they are."

Suddenly his expression changed, his voice dropped, his lips twisted, and he let out a hoarse, stuttering laugh. His knees began to shake and he pinched his mouth. "I'm surprised at you, Nurse Adeh," he said, "after all, you are an intelligent woman. You should be more careful about what you say. How can you believe something which doesn't make any sense. How can you say that your hospital possesses a book containing the history of Gumlidata. Gumlidata was destroyed in the days of the first Gothic invasions. And you say that a book from these ancient times has come down to our day, and the old people in the hospital have read it. Now really, my dear nurse, how can you reconcile this kind of nonsense with simple reality? How could a book like this ever get to the hospital . . . to the hospital which you, my dear nurse, serve so well. . . . How? How? Pardon me, my dear Adinah, if I tell you that this is a very doubtful story. You have heard a silly old folk tale and it has enchanted you with its romance. Or perhaps you have confused Gumlidata with . . . with . . . I don't know with what city you might have confused Gumlidata. What did you hear about this manuscript? How did it get to the hospital? You have made me curious, my dear lady, very curious for more information. I feel just like a psychoanalyst. Aren't you surprised at me, the author of a book myself, being so curious about someone else's book? It's not enough that my house is filled with books, I must go looking for others. Let me tell you, just between us, all these books in my cabinet are not there for reading, they're there for effect. And if you want, I'll tell you the real reason: self-preservation. People see the books and start talking about them, and I don't have to discuss my own work with them. Please tell me, though, how did this history of Gumlidata ever get to your hospital?"

"I haven't read the book," answered the nurse Adeh Eden, "and when it was taken out of the reading room some time ago I forgot it. I don't devote much time to books generally. When I come to your house for books, it's not for myself, of course, but for the sake of my good people, in order to ease their suffering. Sometimes books can do that. As for the parchment pages, I remember how surprised I was when I first saw them about forty years ago—like most nurses, I had to know everything about every article I saw where I worked. An old man noticed that the volume of parchment interested me and he told me what he had heard about the book. I still remember a little of what he said. If old age hasn't confused my memory, I'll try to pass on his story. May I sit down and tell you what I heard?"

Amzeh was suddenly embarrassed. "My God!" he cried out in confusion. "How could I let you stand all this time! Sit down, do sit down . . . here, on this chair. Not that one, this chair over here . . . it is the most comfortable one in my house. Please sit down and tell me your story."

The old woman sat down in the chair that he brought her, gathered up the folds of her dress, clasped her hands together, and, taking a deep breath, began. "As far as I can remember, this is the story. After the Gothic hordes had conquered the great city of Gumlidata and reduced its strength to dust, they found the tyrant ruler of the city, Count Gifayon Glaskinon Gitra'al, of the house of Giara'al, just as he was about to flee. He moaned and wept and pleaded for his life, asking that he be made a slave to their nation and their king, Alaric. The Goths allowed him to live, and carried him off with them as a slave. He had with him a history which contained stories of the city's might and valor, stories that used to be read before the time of Alaric the King. On the way he fell sick, and the Goths left him for dead and went on. He wandered about in the fields until some lepers, who were following the soldiers for scraps of food and clothing, came upon him. They took pity on him, released him from his chains, and nursed him until he regained his health. He soon realized who his saviors were and began to groan and curse, declaring that death was better than life with the lepers. For in those days a leper was looked upon as a dead man and anyone who came in contact with an untouchable was himself considered to be infected. They tried to comfort him by saying that if he went away he might fall into the hands of the Goths and their allies who would surely kill him, or else he might be waylaid by roving packs of wild beasts who would surely eat him alive; but if he stayed with them he would be saved from the punishments of both men and beasts and have food to sustain him. They took him to their camp and gave him a bundle of straw to carry, so that if he were approached by a healthy man he might warn him away by shaking the straw, and they hung a small cup about his neck, for merciful people would sometimes throw scraps of food to the sick.

"He lived with them for some time, eating what they ate and drinking what they drank. He saw how well they treated him and began to repay them in kind. On long winter nights he would read to them from his book, entertaining them with stories of the great city of Gumlidata and tales of his ancestors, the tyrant counts who governed over Gumlidata and its dependencies. In time, both the Count and his benefactors died. No trace remained of them except the book. Men live and die, but their instruments remain and live on. The Count's friends died, but their place was taken by a new generation. They discovered the book and read it from cover to cover, joining their tears to those of the first generation. After many generations the world began to change and people began to realize how great was the suffering of the lepers, how difficult and terrible their ordeal. Not only was their sickness a great tribulation, but they were forced to live in forests and deserts and wander about in search of food. And there were times during the hard winter days when they had no sustenance and were unable to beg for food and they simply died of starvation. Eventually, benevolent groups were formed and a shelter established for the lepers, where they were brought together and their needs taken care of. Herr Doctor, I doubt whether there is anyone else in the world who knows more than I have told you about these sheets of parchment. But you want to leave. I hope you aren't late for your appointment."

"No, I'm not late for my appointment," answered Adiel Amzeh. "In fact, this is only the beginning of my appointment. Take a little more time, sit a little while longer, and we'll fill our hands with books and take them to the good people. Sit where you are, Nurse, sit a while and forget about my book. My book is used to waiting." Amzeh went over to the cabinets lining his walls and began to take books down. When he had accumulated a large pile, he tied them up in packages. He took down more books, muttering: "They'll enjoy them, they'll enjoy these books." Several times he repeated the process, searching and ransacking his shelves, whispering and muttering all the time, "What shall I give? What shall I give?" If the old woman had not stayed his hand, he would have taken all his books from their shelves and given them to her.

"You take a bundle and I'll take a bundle," he said when he had finished, "and we'll deliver them to your patients. As for Mr. . . . as for Mr. what's-his-name . . . Mr. Goldenthal, Gebhard Goldenthal, who is waiting for me to come, well, I'm sure he will find something else to occupy himself with. And now, my dear Adeh Eden, let's hurry so that we arrive before the sun sets, and you will open the gate for me and take me to see the book—the book of which you have spoken. What's the matter, Nurse? Why do you make such a face? Don't you think they'll allow me to enter? We'll swear that I'm going to visit my mother, and if they don't let me in I'll lie down on the steps of the hospital and won't move an inch until they say I can enter. Are you unhappy? Are you sorry about something? If it's because of me, don't be sorry. This is the most glorious day of my life, sweeter than any day I have ever lived, and what you have told me is sweeter than anything I have ever heard since . . . since . . . I'm really confused now, I don't know since when. Look, look, it's already going down. I mean the sun, the sun. The sun is more beautiful when it sets than when it rises. For twenty years a man must be hidden in the sun's shadow in order to be able to utter such a simple piece of wisdom."

They went out of the city, the two of them walking together, Amzeh in long strides, the old woman with short steps. He chattered as he walked; she managed every so often to bring forth a word which sounded more like a sigh. Everyone who passed by and recognized her stepped aside, and she avoided them as well; she knew these people were afraid of her and was careful not to arouse any unnecessary terror. But Adiel Amzeh was not conscious of the passers-by avoiding them as they went along. He turned to his companion suddenly. "Do you remember whether I locked the door?" he asked. He put down his package and saw that the key was still in his hand. "I'm carrying the key with the package and am not conscious of what I'm doing," he said with a laugh. "It's because of the heaviness of the burden I have to bear." For a minute he was silent. Then he cried out, "My God!" with a mixture of impatience and reproach, for at the edge of his consciousness he saw himself reading the book of Gumlidata in the hospital and the faded words on the parchment prevented him from progressing quickly. Because of this book, too, he had forgotten his own book which he had worked on for twenty years, and he had forgotten Mr. Goldenthal who had agreed to publish it. After about an hour's walk, they arrived at the lepers' hospital.

I don't know through which gate they entered or how much time it took before he was granted admittance. And I can't describe the condition of the book itself, which was so covered with pus that even the lepers felt a loathing for it. I don't know all the details and have no love for suppositions. Let me put aside the doubtful and come back to what is certain.

Amzeh came to the house of the untouchables and after much argument he finally was allowed to enter. He went in and they tied him in an antiseptic apron which reached from his neck to his feet. They took the book out of the chest it was stored in, and gave it to him with a warning not to touch it. Amzeh stared at it until his eyes seemed to occupy half his face. He looked at it for a long time, then jumped up quickly to open it. They took hold of him and told him to wait. He was fitted with a pair of white gloves which they carefully tied so they would not fall off. Then they warned him again not to touch the book unless his hands were protected with gloves. They told him that only a simpleminded man would neglect such a warning. I don't know whether he heard them or not. This I do know: his eyes grew so large they seemed to cover his entire face—and half his neck as well. When they saw that he had somewhat regained his composure, they left, providing him with a place in the hospital garden among the trees which are known as the "Trees of Eden." Adiel Amzeh sat there and painstakingly read every letter, every word, column, and page which the book contained, the caretaker standing by his side and turning the pages as he progressed. For they were still afraid he was so excited that he would not exercise the necessary restraint. The book had been touched by the hands of many untouchables, and it seemed almost as if it were not written on parchment, but on the skin of a leper, and not ink but pus had been used to inscribe the words.

What more can I say? After he had carefully gone over every sentence in the book, he found the answer to the riddle that had troubled him for many years: how Gumlidata had been conquered, from which side of the city the first bands of the Goths had entered. For Gumlidata had been surrounded by a solid wall of stone and protected on all sides by natural fortifications. And so within a few short hours Amzeh solved the problem that had caused him so much trouble during his years of exhaustive research. For your sake, my friends, and for the sake of the whole House of Israel, let me tell you the story the dead words told our scholar. I'll try to summarize what was written there at great length.

The book of parchment told the story of one of the Hun women, a young girl named Geldag or Eldag, who one day left the camp of the Huns, the allies of the Goths, and rode about on a wild ass. She reached the cisterns behind the city of Gumlidata where she was caught and brought to the city. The servants of the tyrant, the old Count Gifayon Glaskinon Gitra'al of the house of Giara'al, grandfather of the young Count Gifayon Glaskinon Gitra'al Giara'al, noticed her and brought her for a gift to their master. She was horrified by the old man and his city, disgusted by his groaning and drooling, his narrow bed and his strange manners, and nauseated by the smell of the city and its sacrificial altars. She tried to flee at once, but was caught and returned to the Count. The same thing happened three or four times; each time she was caught. Finally, she saw that escape was impossible and she sat brooding how to gain revenge on her captors.

At about the same time the girl was held captive, the Goths, with Gaditon the Brave at their head, rose up and waged war with Gumlidata. The city's inhabitants held the Goths in great terror, for they knew that every place the barbarians conquered they slaughtered and burned, and if Gumlidata was vanquished, their future was annihilation. The tyrant Count saw that his city was cut off from all help, and he fell into a deep, sorrowful melancholy. Had it not been for Eldag, the Hun girl, who had changed her ways and begun to show him a love and devotion he had known with no other woman, he probably would have died of his sorrow before the Goths had a chance to hang him.

When the court guards saw that Eldag had changed her attitude toward the Count, they ceased watching her as carefully as before. Eldag took advantage of the guards' carelessness and began to take long walks through the city, wandering about everywhere. She even visited the city wall near the Valley of the Cranes, which most people avoided for fear that it might collapse. Years before, an earthquake had struck the city and shaken the wall in several places. The citizens of Gumlidata were careful not to bother Eldag, for they knew that only the power of her charms had saved their king from melancholy. So enamored of the girl was their king that he had his tailors make her a mantle as a gift, a kind of priestly garment normally worn by a queen, woven with bands of calves' eyes arranged in the shape of the Valley of the Cranes.

One day Eldag remained in the king's garden, playing with her wild ass among the tall trees. This ass was one of many animals in the garden, each of which had suckled at a woman's breast. For there was a strange custom in Gumlidata. If a woman conceived and it was not known who the father was, her relatives waited until she gave birth and then took the infant and brought it to these animals to be suckled. They looked for an animal that had recently given birth, and left the infant to be weaned, taking the animal's young to the human mother for suckling. If they could not find the young of a tame animal, they brought her the young of a wild one. They were most careful about the children of the noblewomen, *Givyatans* in their language, for if a noblewoman had given birth and the father was unknown, the infant was killed and the young of an animal was brought to the mother, so that her noble blood would not be mixed with the blood of the common people.

So Eldag played with her pet in the garden among the tall trees. She was quite unafraid of animals, having spent most of her life with them: her father, Gichul the Clown, was the owner of a dancing bear. A young ass saw them and began snorting and hee-hawing, as if in reproach. Eldag heard the young animal's cries. "An ass always sounds like an ass," she said with a laugh, "even if it has been suckled by a duchess. What is it you want? Do you want this mantle which covers my heart? Come and I will wrap round your neck an ornament more beautiful than any that has been worn by your noble wet-nurse." The young ass heard her and came close. She took her mantle from her bosom and tied it about the animal's throat, and made him bow his head as if in thanks, as she had seen Gothic noblemen do when they received gifts.

Suddenly the girl was overwhelmed with a deep longing for her home, her family, and her people. She was filled with a burning rage and her anger turned against the ass who had reminded her of her former happiness. She was angry at the ass because he was more faithful than she was: even after she had placed the gift around his neck, the ass continued to groan. She grabbed hold of him by the ears in order to strike him. The calves' eyes which had been woven into the mantle in the shape of the Valley of Cranes shone before her. Her heart began to beat wildly. She tried to gain control of herself so that she would not cry out and give away her plan. She forced herself to smile and dragged the ass to the city wall near the Valley of Cranes; there, she found the place which had collapsed during the earthquake and had not been completely repaired. She broke through the opening and pushed the ass with the mantle around his neck outside. And Eldag was happy, for she knew that if the Goths saw the ass, they would understand he had been sent as a sign that they should enter the city through the Valley of Cranes. She controlled her joy and returned to the old Count, assuming a happy countenance for him, his court, and his city. So charmed was the population by Eldag's grace and beauty that they forgot about the Gothic soldiers who were besieging their city.

The ass went out of the city and reached a nearby forest. His nose sniffed the odors of trees and flowers and he began to snort loudly like a wild ass who has returned to his home. The noise was heard by some Gothic soldiers. They were surprised to see the ass with the mantle around his neck, for they had never seen an animal adorned like this. They brought the animal to Gaditon, their general. Gaditon the Brave saw the mantle. "Is there a place known as the Valley of the Cranes?" he asked his soldiers. "Is there one of our people in Gumlidata?" Gichul the Clown was brought to the general, and he told him that his daughter had disappeared. He saw the ass and the strange ornament it wore, and he knew that it was his daughter's work. The Goths sent soldiers to inspect the wall near the Valley of Cranes, and when they saw the place through which Eldag had sent the ass, the Goths entered the city. They set the city on fire, killing everyone in their path: old and young, infant and aged, male and female. Not a man or woman was left alive except Eldag, the Hun girl, who was released from her bondage, and the grandson of the old Count who was made a slave. . . .

All this was written on the last page of the book as a kind of epilogue by the author. And when Adiel Amzeh read the story, his eyes shed many tears. How great is the true writer, he thought, who does not abandon his work even when the sword of death hangs over his neck, who writes with his very blood what his eyes have seen!

Adiel Amzeh read many other things in the book. There were pages which supported some of his theories, and there were other pages which completely contradicted what he had previously thought. It seems he had relied too much on earlier scholars, even though he realized that much of what they wrote was confused. Adiel Amzeh remained at the hospital throughout the summer reading the book. When the days grew colder and the land was covered with frost, he had to stop working outside. He took a room at the hospital and had a heater brought in. He sat there studying the text, joining letter to letter and word to word until he could read whole passages without trouble. And if he discovered something unusual he would read the passage aloud to the patients in the great hall. "My friends and brothers," he would say, "listen while I read to you." And he would read to them about the people of the great city of Gumlidata, who had been a mighty nation, full of pride and valor, until the Gothic hordes conquered them and reduced the city to dust and ashes. He would tell them about Gomesh and Gutz and Gush and Guach, the gods of Gumlidata, and about its apostates, its great temples, its priests—each one named according to its function. And sometimes Adiel Amzeh would tell them about his new theories. He had thought out many new hypotheses and some of them he had noted on the parchment book. But his book never reached the hands of the living, for it was forbidden to remove any article or letter or book from the lepers' house. Nevertheless, in some way or other, some of his new ideas became known to his colleagues. Many times, when Adeh Eden had brought from his house the scientific journals which he received regularly, he would read his ideas in articles signed by others. He was shocked that something which he had worked on so long and hard was now published under another scholar's signature. "If this kind of thing can happen," he would ask himself, "then why do I work? I ought to be satisfied with what the others say."

Yet learning bestows a special blessing on those who are not put off so easily. Yes, Adiel Amzeh would ask himself for what and for whom he was working. But the Goddess of Wisdom herself would take hold of him and whisper: "Sit, my love, sit and do not leave me." So he would sit and discover new things which had been unknown to all the learned men of the ages until he came and revealed them. And since there were many things and learning is endless and there is much to discover and investigate and understand, he did not put his work aside and did not leave the hospital and he remained there forevermore.

—Translated by Joel Blocker